PLINY

THE ROMAN WORLD SERIES

GENERAL EDITOR: F. KINCHIN SMITH, M.A.
Senior Lecturer in Classics, University of London Institute of Education

PLINY
Selections from the Letters
Edited by C. E. Robinson

CATULLUS
Selections from the Poems
Edited by F. Kinchin Smith and T. W. Melluish

VERGIL
Selections from the Eclogues, Georgics and Aeneid
Edited by W. F. Jackson Knight

POETRY AND PROSE
A Selection from the less familiar Latin Writers
Edited by Barbara J. Hodge and F. Kinchin Smith

Opinions
on the Series expressed by Senior Classics
Masters and Mistresses

" . . . wholly admirable, interesting, cheap and full of the social background which most texts so sadly lack."—*Grammar School*

"I consider the edition of Pliny a good one. ... the Catullus possibly the most admirable edition of a classical author for schools that I have seen."—*Public School*

"I am most impressed."—*Girls' High School*

"They are the most attractive editions that I know."—*University Professor*

"A delightful book; pleasant to hold and read."—GREECE AND ROME

"Wholly delightful."—JOURNAL OF EDUCATION

"Gives everything that a Latin text book should offer."—AMA

PLINY

*Selections from the
Letters*

EDITED BY

C. E. ROBINSON M.A.

Assistant Master at Winchester College

LONDON
GEORGE ALLEN & UNWIN LTD
MUSEUM STREET

FIRST PUBLISHED IN	1939
SECOND IMPRESSION	1947
THIRD IMPRESSION	1948
FOURTH IMPRESSION	1951
FIFTH IMPRESSION	1956
SIXTH IMPRESSION	1958
SEVENTH IMPRESSION	1963
EIGHTH IMPRESSION	1965
NINTH IMPRESSION	1966
TENTH IMPRESSION	1968
ELEVENTH IMPRESSION	1969
TWELFTH IMPRESSION	1970

ISBN 0 04 876001 3

PRINTED IN GREAT BRITAIN
BY ROBERT MACLEHOSE & CO LTD
GLASGOW

CONTENTS

*The references to the traditional text of Pliny's Letters are given
in brackets at the end of each extract*

GENERAL INTRODUCTION

Twenty-five pages of Caesar or Cicero, and five hundred lines of Ovid or Vergil, are a poor return for four years of Latin, yet this is all that most of the 30,000[1] or so boys and girls in England and Wales, who annually take the School Certificate, read of Latin literature. If they continued their studies further and read some Catullus, Lucretius or Tacitus, this meagre pre-School-Certificate diet might be excusable, but less than 10 per cent. continue the study of Latin beyond that examination. It is as if we taught a French boy English for four years and gave him nothing to read except twenty-five pages of Wellington's dispatches or of a speech of Burke, and five hundred lines of *Paradise Lost*. No Shakespeare, Keats or Tennyson—no plays or lyric poetry. The idea of the Roman World Series is to give these 30,000 pupils first-hand acquaintance with more of the great literature of Rome before they ' drop ' Latin for ever.

The time has come for a different orientation in the teaching of Latin. The aim of Latin teaching should be the understanding and appreciation of Latin literature. Reading must be wider and more intelligent. There must be more study of what the Romans did and felt and said when they were not fighting. ' The great pagan civilisations march their eternal round ', said the late Sir Walter Raleigh, ' like weary ghosts through the schoolroom ; at the stroke of the clock they vanish, and the activities of real life are resumed. Hardly does the thought occur that these too, like other restless spirits, have a message to deliver, and are burning to speak.' That there are Roman writers besides Caesar, Cicero and Ovid, burning to speak, and intelligible with the right help to the young, is the belief behind this series.

The first three volumes consist of selections from Pliny's letters and the poetry of Catullus and Vergil. It is hoped to produce further volumes on the same lines, of authors chosen for the interest of their subject-matter to the modern world. As Mr. C. E. Robinson says in his introduction to the first volume of this series, ' the Modern World is nearer to the Ancient World than

[1] e.g. 29,386 offered Latin in 1945

7

to the period which lies between.' From answers to a questionnaire sent recently to certain schools, it was found that Pliny was the least read of Latin authors, but when read the most popular. His letters deal with a period of Roman history that is more interesting and important to us to-day than any other. His style, if more sophisticated, is less involved than Caesar's, and difficulties will diminish through the interest of what he has to say.

The second volume introduces a poet who was as human as Burns, as unashamed in love as Donne, and as frank as modern poets in expressing what he felt and thought. At present Catullus is rarely read before the School Certificate examination, but when a boy or girl does make acquaintance with ' the tenderest of Roman poets nineteen hundred years ago ' it may be an experience that will last a lifetime. Much of Catullus is harder than Ovid, but some is easier, and most is more interesting.

The third volume is *Vergil for Pleasure*, by W. F. Jackson Knight. Vergil, according to Christopher Hollis, is ' one of the very small company whom it is necessary to understand if one is going to understand anything.' This is planned as a book to be read straight through by those who sincerely wish to share, with millions of their predecessors, the wonder of Vergil's ' ocean-roll of rhythm ', and the wisdom which ' human grandeur's most exalted voice ' can impart. The book is arranged as a continuous story built on passages from Vergil himself (his *Eclogues* and *Georgics* as well as the *Æneid*) and the English poetry he has inspired. The book contains much which will be new even to those who know their Vergil well ; the fruits of the most recent research and of many years devoted to the study of Vergil.

In the text of these volumes difficulties are reduced where necessary by omissions, but not by alteration of the original words. In the belief that knowledge of background should be acquired through the reading of authors themselves, rather than from ' cram ' books on antiquities, the text is interwoven with English commentary on relevant aspects of Roman life, history and literature. The notes, printed at the bottom of the page to assist rapid reading in class, stress the cultural not less than the linguistic side. Explanations of syntactical points are left mainly to the teacher.

F. KINCHIN SMITH

HISTORICAL INTRODUCTION

THE Modern World is nearer to the Ancient World than to the period which lies between. The Middle Ages baffle us with their ecstasies and despairs, their high spiritual ideals and crude superstitions, their extraordinary energy and still more extraordinary ignorance. The Romans, on the other hand, we can more nearly understand. They expressed their thoughts and emotions in terms which are intelligible to our minds. If Pliny heard of a friend's death or felt dissatisfied with his own conduct, he sat down and wrote a lucid and well-reasoned letter about it ; he did not order masses to be said for the dead man's soul or go off on pilgrimage for the salvation of his own. Even from a material point of view, his world had much in common with ours. Its standard of domestic comfort was high. Living-rooms were fitted with ' central heating '. Bathing-arrangements outdid those of any modern private house. Travel was easy ; for the Romans were incomparable road-makers. The journey from Italy to Britain then took less time than it did at the beginning of Victoria's reign. There was a system of post-chaises, working in relays, along all the main routes. Correspondence between friends passed freely. Pliny sometimes wrote to his wife twice in a day. Even the topics covered in his letters have a modern ring : Do ghosts exist ? Shall we form a fire-brigade? Is the popular enthusiasm for sport misplaced? Striking, however, is the absence of any really vital issue. Such political excitements as Pliny mentions seem very tame affairs. He never suggests that the state of the world could in any way be improved. Still less did it strike him that the Empire's safety could be seriously menaced.

It had not always been so. A hundred years before Pliny's time Rome had nearly foundered in a terrible political crisis. This had resulted from a breakdown of the old form of government. For many centuries the affairs of the Republic had been managed by the Senate, assisted by consuls and other elected magistrates. But step by step she had been conquering the Mediterranean world, and, as her Empire grew larger, the Senate's capacity to deal with it grew less. Wars, fought either for its increase or protection, brought great generals to the fore ; and these generals began to fight for the supremacy of the State—first Marius was defeated by Sulla, then Pompey by Julius Caesar, and finally Mark Antony by the man who was destined to lay the permanent foundations of the imperial system—Augustus.

For by now it was clear that the problems of the Roman Empire could only be solved, if its direction passed from the Senate's hands into the hands of a single ruler. Nowadays we should call Augustus a dictator ; but, like some modern dictators, he did not make a clean sweep of the past. Just as Hitler preserved (in form at least) the German Parliament or Reichstag, and Mussolini the monarchy of Italy, so Augustus maintained much of the old Republican constitution. He kept the Senate and he kept the magistrates. But the government of the Empire required, as we have said, the direction of a single brain. So, whether Augustus and his successors wished it or no, the Senate faded imperceptibly into the background. The magistrates, though still annually elected at the capital, ceased to be of real importance. What mattered were the men who commanded the legions and ruled the provinces ; and it became inevitable that these should be responsible to the Emperor and the Emperor alone.

So great indeed was the Emperor's power that his subjects came to regard him with superstitious awe, as something more than human. In his own lifetime altars and shrines were erected to Augustus. On death he was formally deified ; and the same honours were paid to others after him. This was the more remarkable since his immediate successors were far from worthy. Tiberius, the first, was efficient, but his nerve broke under the strain. The next, Caligula, was mad. Claudius was under the thumb of his favourites. Nero's misrule was so gross that it provoked a military rebellion. Thus, when Pliny was a boy of eight, the throne became vacant ; and once again Italy was the cock-pit of fierce civil wars between rival generals. Victory went to Vespasian ; and with his accession the Empire entered on a new phase of its history.

Previous emperors had all been aristocrats, related in one degree or another to Augustus himself. Vespasian was of the middle class, a tough, hard-working man of business. He ruled the Empire on more efficient lines. His staff of secretaries had to rise at cock-crow. He promoted to official posts, whether at home or in the provinces, men of energy and ideals, such as Pliny's uncle and Agricola, the governor of Britain. Such methods set a new standard for his successors. His two sons, it is true, scarcely lived up to them ; for Titus was too easy-going, Domitian too suspicious and tyrannical. But the latter's death and Nerva's accession prepared the way for a new type of Emperor. Nerva himself had been raised to the throne because the Senate thought him suitable ; and he in his turn appointed as his heir the best man he could discover. His choice fell on Trajan, and it proved a sound one. Trajan had been trained as a military commander and he spent much of his reign on the frontiers. None the less he found time to attend to every department of public administration. He knew how to be affable to his subordinates, but, as his letters to Pliny show, he knew also how to maintain the dignity of his position. To his favour and encouragement Pliny himself owed much. He had begun his public career under Domitian and Nerva, passing through the regular course of magistracies at Rome. But it was in Trajan's reign that he rose to the forefront of affairs, becoming a member of the Emperor's Privy Council, and being sent out on a special mission to reform a mismanaged province. The two men were on terms of close intimacy. ' My very dear Secundus ' Trajan called him in his letters. Trajan was an exacting master; for there were no details so small but he liked to be kept informed of them. But he was an inspiring master too. He had a strong pride in the high standards of public life. ' That would be unworthy of our age ' he wrote to Pliny, when the latter was wondering whether to listen to a charge made in an anonymous letter by a malicious provincial.

Trajan's pride was justified. His reign was probably the high water mark of the Empire's prosperity. Into all the lands which Rome conquered, she had carried her culture, her comforts, her methods of orderly life. Go from the Great Wall on the Northumbrian border to the oasis-city of Palmyra beyond Damascus ; go from the fortresses of the Danubian frontier to the city of Timgad on the fringe of the Sahara ; and everywhere you will still find evidence of her occupation—remains of towns laid out, after her manner, on a regular chess-board pattern, with straight intersecting streets and central market-squares, with temples and town-halls, amphitheatres and aqueducts. Roman speech and Roman habits went hand in hand with this material civilisa-tion. Rights of Roman citizenship were gradually extended, till at length every freeborn inhabitant of the Empire could one day claim the privilege. Over all peace reigned. ' The whole world keeps holiday ', wrote an author born at this time. ' Strife is stilled, leaving only the rivalry of cities, each striving to be the fairest and most beautiful. Every city is full of gymnasia, fountains, porticos and temples. The whole earth is adorned as if it were a garden.'

Little wonder that the Romans were proud of their achieve-ment. But, at this very moment, unheeded by them, the first symptoms of the Empire's decay were making their appearance. Agriculture was failing to keep pace with the growing needs of the luxurious cities. The soil was becoming exhausted. The Romans lacked the spirit of initiative which might have produced a scientific remedy ; and, though efforts were made to bring new land under the plough, a decline of production set in. Meanwhile on the frontiers in both north and east, barbarian enemies were beginning their slow but relentless pressure. Trajan himself spent many years of his reign beyond the Danube fighting the Dacians. Huge armies were needed to man the threatened points ; and the burden of feeding these served further to impoverish the tillers of the soil. Thus, as the pressure from without increased, so also did the strain of maintaining life within ; and the fabric of the Empire began ominously to crack. Once again civil wars grew frequent and rival claimants for the throne exhausted strength which was sorely needed against the external foe. First one province and then another went down before the barbarians. At last, in 410 A.D., Italy was overrun and Rome sacked. While at Constantinople emperors continued to rule over the eastern provinces, the West was given over to anarchy. Civilisation vanished. The Dark Ages set in.

Nevertheless what Rome had done was not wholly lost or wasted. She understood, as no other people had understood, how to organise civilised life under the rule of law and justice ; and even in the chaos of the centuries which followed, the lesson was not forgotten. In Gaul especially the customs which she had taught her subjects were taken over by the barbarian settlers and became the basis of Frankish government. The Catholic Church itself, the most influential institution in Europe, was modelled upon the Roman political system. At its head was a single and all-powerful figure—the Pope. Acting (like the Senate) as advisers to the Pope was the body of Cardinals.[1] Over the separate dioceses [2] Bishops ruled like provincial governors. In short, the whole tradition of ecclesiastical discipline was Roman to the core and in the Papal church it remains so to this day.

[1] The Pope and his Cardinals sitting in council, are actually known as the ' Curia ', the Latin name of the Senate House.

[2] ' Dioceses ' was a name given to a group of provinces under the late Empire.

Meanwhile, as years went on, the kings who in various countries sought to curb unruly barons and impose order on turbulent subjects, looked likewise to the model of Rome ; and their reforms were founded on a study of Roman law and Roman administration. Indeed throughout the Middle Ages men continued to look back, with a certain wistfulness, to the Golden Age of settled life which Europe had once enjoyed. Such books as they possessed were practically confined to the works of Roman authors preserved in the libraries of monasteries ; and, being unliterary themselves, they felt an exaggerated respect for whatever was written down. So they drank in eagerly the wisdom of the ancients, and not unnaturally concluded that, if order was once again to be brought out of chaos, it must be by the methods of Imperial Rome.

What then were the principles for which the Empire stood? Two stand out. First there was the principle of centralised authority. At the head of all stood the Emperor, alone, absolute, answerable to none. From him all authority proceeded : being delegated first to his subordinates and by them to others again. ' I also am a man under authority,' said the centurion of the Gospel, ' I say to one " Go " and he goeth ; to another " Come " and he cometh.' There could be no more vivid summary of the Imperial system. Contrast with this the principle of a modern democracy. The ' Prime Minister ' of England is the ' First Servant ' of the people, not their master ; he is answerable to Parliament and Parliament is dependent upon the electors. Authority proceeds, in other words, from below upwards, not downwards from above. Hitler would doubtless have said that he too was the people's representative ; but for all that the Nazi system was more akin to the Roman than to ours. Whether in the long run democracy will prove the more efficient or more permanent, time alone will reveal.

But there was a second principle which served in some degree to counterbalance the first—the Rights of the Individual. From the remotest days the Romans had always shown a great respect for the sanctity of law. Even to the folk they conquered they accorded legal rights; for provincials were permitted to prosecute their governors, and orators like Pliny were ready to come forward and support them in the courts. Every individual citizen, high or low, rich or poor, was equal before the law. There was no discrimination between class or creed or race. Even a Jew of Tarsus, as we know from the New Testament, could rely on a fair trial; and, if he appealed to the Emperor's judgment seat, to the Emperor he was sent. Strict impartiality was the ideal and, on the whole, the practice of Roman judge and juror; and they were proud of it. It took time of course to perfect their legal system; but, as time went on, the abstract principles of justice, which underlay the practice of their courts, were defined by expert jurists. Under Trajan's successor, Hadrian, a comprehensive code was made, clearing up obscurities and bringing inconsistent laws into line with one another. The work of codification continued; and it did not reach its final form until in the sixth century A.D. Justinian, the Emperor of Constantinople, issued his famous ' Digest '. In his code we find the clearest statement of the abstract principles of justice—as, for instance, that ' No man may be judge in his own case ', ' No appeal for mercy shall be made while the case is being tried ', and even that ' it befits the Monarch to declare himself bound by the law '.

In the Middle Ages, when Europe was feeling its way back to order and civilisation, the influence of these Roman codes was very great. Later still, Napoleon, when he remade the laws of France, went back to them for a model; and even at the present day, lawyers still study them. Roman Law, in fact, is a vital element in the European tradition; and violation of its principles for political ends is an ominous symptom of the breakdown of our civilisation. In many foreign countries to-day political opinions, not the facts of the case, have become the test of guilt or innocence. The murder of opponents has been approved or condemned according as its authors were for the government or against it. There has been one law for 'Aryans' and another for Jews; and imprisonment without trial is too common to provoke comment. In such countries, in short, the rights of the individual are no longer recognised; and thus the conception of justice, inherited from Rome and developed by western nations for over two thousand years, has been destroyed in far fewer days.

Enough has been said to show that the Modern World owes much to its Roman heritage; but there remains one element of that heritage more important perhaps than all others—language. Latin—the dialect of Italian speech employed in the plain of Latium which surrounded Rome—has a history infinitely longer than the thousand years or so of her national history. In Italy, France and Spain it was developed, by a slow process of transformation, into the languages which are there spoken to this day. In its purer form it remained and still remains the language of the Papal Church, which even now repeats its services and 'Pater Nosters' in the tongue of the first Roman Christians. Throughout the Middle Ages it was the language of scholars and lawyers, historians and diplomatists. At the Renaissance, when men found the Anglo-French of earlier writers inadequate to express the multitude of new ideas which were surging up in their minds, they borrowed freely from the Latin, coining new words as scientists and inventors are still coining them to-day. More than this, the influence of Latin authors made a deep impression upon the style of English authors, especially during the second half of the seventeenth century and the first half of the eighteenth. Some scholars have wished to free our speech from such classical encumbrances and get back to the vocabulary of Anglo-Saxon origin. But this is a foolish and impossible ideal. For better or for worse the Latin language has given us something which is now an essential part of our mental make-up; and without some study of its formation and its idiom there can be no genuine understanding of our native literature nor perhaps even command of our native speech.

Most travellers in Northern Italy know Como. It is a
beauty-spot, famous for its soft luminous sunshine, its
shimmering mountains and, nestling among them, its
exquisite blue lake. It was here at the little town of Novum
Comum or New Como, some twenty miles from Milan, that
Caius Plinius Caecilius Secundus was born in the winter of
61-62 A.D. How well he loved the place is shown by the
following extract from a letter he wrote to a friend who lived
there. A Roman's taste in scenery was somewhat different
from our own. He tended to admire what man had done to
improve on nature even more than nature itself; so that it
may be noted here how in his list of the mansion's charms
the lake actually comes fifth.

I Quid agit Comum, tuae meaeque deliciae? [1] Quid
suburbanum [2] amoenissimum? Quid illa porticus [3] verna
semper? Quid platanon [4] opacissimus? Quid euripus [5]
viridis et gemmeus? Quid subjectus lacus? Quid illa
mollis et tamen solida gestatio? [6] Quid balineum illud, quod
plurimus sol implet et circumit? [I 3]

❡ When Pliny was barely fifteen his father died, and he
passed under the care of two guardians. One of these was
his uncle, known to history as the Elder Pliny. This man
was a ' character', if ever there was one. Though abnormally
stout and subject to asthma, he was possessed of untiring
energy. Work, as the saying goes, was meat and drink to

---

[1] ' delight ' or ' favourite '.
[2] ' house on the outskirts of a town '.   [3] ' verandah '.
[4] ' grove of plane-trees '.   [5] ' canal ' or ' conduit '.
[6] ' a promenade used for exercise '.

him. He was a walking encyclopedia of knowledge. He had written books of prodigious length on all manner of subjects. They were not works of any great originality. Much of his material was collected from other authors. In the course of compiling his *Natural History* he is said to have consulted as many as two thousand books ; and as he read, he copied out passages which specially interested him. He made his young nephew do the same, and it is not difficult to see that on a boy of Pliny's age the effect of associating with such a man must have been profound. Here is Pliny's own description of his uncle's habits.

II Pergratum est mihi quod tam diligenter libros avunculi mei lectitas, ut habere omnes velis quaerasque qui sint omnes. Fungar indicis partibus [1] atque etiam quo sint ordine scripti notum tibi faciam.

> De jaculatione equestri unus
> De vita Pomponi Secundi duo
> Bellorum Germaniae viginti
> Dubii sermonis octo [2]
> A fine Aufidi Bassi triginta unus [a]
> Naturae historiarum triginta septem.

Miraris quod tot volumina [b] homo occupatus absolverit. Sed erat acre ingenium, incredibile studium, summa vigilantia. Lucubrare Vulcanalibus [c] incipiebat, hieme ab hora septima, saepe sexta.[d] Ante lucem ibat ad Vespasianum imperatorem (nam ille quoque noctibus utebatur), inde ad delegatum sibi officium. Reversus domum, quod reliquum temporis, studiis reddebat. Post cibum saepe jacebat in sole, liber legebatur ; adnotabat excerpebatque. Nihil enim legit quod non excerperet ; dicere etiam solebat nullum esse librum tam malum ut non aliqua parte prodesset. Post

[1] ' I will perform the function of an index '.
[2] ' eight books (on questions) of doubtful grammar, i.e. problems of language.

solem [e] frigida [3] lavabatur ; deinde gustabat dormiebatque minimum ; mox studebat in cenae tempus. Super hanc liber legebatur, adnotabatur. Memini quemdam ex amicis, cum lector quaedam perperam [4] pronuntiasset, repeti coegisse, huic avunculum meum dixisse ' intellexeras nempe? ' Cum ille adnuisset, ' cur ergo revocabas? decem versus hac tua interpellatione [5] perdidimus.' Tanta erat parsimonia temporis. In secessu solum balinei tempus studiis eximebatur [6] ; nam, dum destringitur tergiturque, audiebat aliquid aut dictabat.

In itinere, quasi solutus ceteris curis, huic uni vacabat: ad latus notarius cum libro et pugillaribus, cujus manus hieme manicis [7] muniebantur, ut ne caeli quidem asperitas ullum studiis tempus eriperet. Repeto me correptum [8] ab eo cur ambularem ; ' poteras ' inquit ' has horas non perdere ' ; nam perire omne tempus arbitrabatur, quod studiis non impenderetur. [III 5]

[a] A history continued from the point where Aufidius Bassus left off.
[b] *Volumen* (from volvo =' roll ') was a roll or scroll of papyrus across which the contents were written in parallel columns.
[c] The *Vulcanalia* or festival of the Fire-God Vulcan took place on August 23rd.
[d] The twelve hours of night were reckoned from sunset (and the twelve hours of day from sunrise). In winter each of these twelve night hours would be longer, in summer shorter—a very awkward scheme.
[e] A ' sun bath ' probably taken naked.

¶ It is difficult to resist the impression that the Elder Pliny was a bit of a prig. His contemporaries may well have thought him so. For even among an industrious people his industry was certainly exceptional. Yet he was no mere literary pedant. He took a leading part in public life and

[3] *frigida* (*aqua*), ' a cold bath '.   [4] ' badly ', ' amiss '.
[5] ' interruption '.
[6] ' only in the privacy of the bath were some moments spared (*lit.* exempted) from study '.
[7] long ' sleeves ' or ' mittens '.   [8] ' taken to task as to why . . .'

filled many official posts, especially in the provinces. The
Emperor Vespasian, as the above extract indicates, consulted him frequently, and amongst other things appointed
him admiral of a naval squadron. His headquarters were at
Misenum, a long promontory which runs out into the sea just
north of the Bay of Naples. Here he was living with his
sister, Pliny's mother, and young Pliny himself, when in
the year 79 A.D. the famous eruption of Mt Vesuvius occurred.
In a letter (from which extracts will be given later) Pliny
described what happened. The admiral sailed across to
rescue some friends at Stabiae whose houses lay close under
the mountain. A strong inshore wind prevented him from
putting out to sea again ; and after a night spent under
terrible circumstances—earthquake shocks, tidal waves, and
a constant rain of cinders from the eruption—he died of
suffocation.

From his uncle Pliny inherited a considerable property ;
and this, combined with the family estates, made him a very
rich man. Besides a town-house at Rome, one country-house
or *villa* in Etruria or Tuscany, another at Beneventum in the
south, and two in the neighbourhood of Como, he also
possessed a magnificent sea-side mansion near the mouth of
the Tiber.   In one of his letters he describes this at length ;
and it will give some idea of the style kept by these Roman
grandees, if we follow him through its numerous apartments.
From the front-door or *vestibulum* we pass first through the
hall or *atrium*, then through a circular cloister or *porticus* and
across a small open court (*area*) into the chief dining-room
overlooking the beach.   Flanking these on the left were the
servants' quarters and a series of bedrooms, one warmed by
a system of flues which introduced hot-air under the floor.
On the right were more bedrooms, several sun-parlours,
alternative dining-rooms, a study which Pliny calls his ' den '
and a sumptuous suite of bathing-rooms, including first the
room where the bather was oiled down (the ancient equivalent of soap), the ' Turkish bath ', the warm swimming
bath, and the cold plunge.   Near these was a yard for ball-

games, a garden full of mulberry and fig-trees, a ' ride ' or
alley with box and rosemary hedges, and a *crypto-porticus* or
gallery ' large enough for a town ', supported on pillars down
the middle and lit by windows on either side.

In the towns, where ground-sites were limited, houses had
to be planned with careful economy of space ; and all the
rooms faced inwards on to central courtyards, outside windows being rare.   In the country ' villa ', on the other hand,
there was no such necessity.   The house could sprawl out
in all directions and windows were placed wherever wanted.
Pliny himself continually insists on the advantageous plan-
ning which secured at once a maximum of sunshine and a
minimum exposure to wind.   Of the furniture he says nothing (to our way of thinking it was probably scanty), nor
does he mention the elaborate decoration of the walls, which
it was then the fashion to cover with painted representations
of landscapes, mythological scenes, etc.   But let the rest of
the description speak for itself in the following paragraphs.
The first tells of a detached wing well away from the rest of
the house.   The second describes the locality of the villa.

III Ante crypto-porticum est xystus, violis odoratus.   In
capite xysti[1] diaeta[2] est, amores mei : ipse posui.   In hac
heliocaminus[3] alia xystum, alia mare, utraque solem
fenestra prospicit.   Junctum est cubiculum.   Non illud
voces servulorum, non maris murmur, non tempestatum
motus, non fulgurum lumen ac ne diem quidem sentit, nisi
fenestris apertis.   In hanc ego diaetam cum me recepi,
abesse mihi etiam a villa mea videor, magnamque voluptatem
praecipue Saturnalibus[a] capio, cum reliqua pars tecti
licentia dierum festisque clamoribus personat : nam nec
ipse meorum lusibus nec illi studiis meis obstrepunt.[4]

Litus ornant varietate gratissima nunc continua, nunc
intermissa tecta villarum, quae praestant multarum urbium
faciem.   Mare non sane pretiosis piscibus abundat, soleas[5]

[1] ' a terrace planted with trees or shrubs '.
[2] ' a living-room or parlour '.
[3] ' sun-parlour '.   [4] ' interrupt '.   [5] ' soles '.

tamen et squillas [6] optimas egerit. Villa vero nostra etiam mediterraneas [7] copias praestat, lac in primis ; nam illuc e pascuis pecora conveniunt, si quando aquam umbramve sectantur. Justisne de causis jam tibi videor incolere, inhabitare, diligere secessum ? Quem tu nimis urbanus [8] es nisi concupiscis. [II 17]

[a] The Festival of Saturn (originally connected with the sowing of crops) took place on December 19th and lasted a week, during which all business came to a standstill. Even slaves were permitted to join in its boisterous festivities. Presents were exchanged, in particular wax-candles and little clay dolls. It may be that the early Christians chose this holiday as a suitable time to keep ' Christmas ' since then even slaves would be free to attend. If this is so, the origin of Christmas-tree candles is easily explained.

❡ The whole of Pliny's house must have covered at least half an acre of ground and seems large for one man and a wife with no children. But we must remember in the first place that, except in one small wing, there was no second storey, and, with this allowance made, the ' villa ' was certainly no larger than many Elizabethan mansions. In the second place a rich Roman kept an enormous staff of servants. Part were slaves, and part were ' freedmen ' or *liberti*, that is, ex-slaves who had been given or had purchased their freedom. Most slaves hailed from Asia Minor or Syria whence they or their parents had been kidnapped and sold in the slave-markets at Delos or Puteoli. Many were of Greek extraction or at any rate of Greek education, and consequently had good wits; and we find freedmen much employed as secretaries, clerks, readers, reciters, entertainers, musicians, and so forth.

A gentleman like Pliny, then, possessed not merely a house ' replete ' (as the modern advertisements say) with every convenience and comfort, but several scores of menials ready to wait on him hand and foot, attend him in the bathroom, carry his sedan-chair, read to him while he dined and in general minister to his needs or pleasures. Yet Pliny, even

[6] ' prawns '.   [7] ' inland '.   [8] ' townee '.

if pampered, was not spoilt by such luxury. Listen to his
description of a summer day spent in his Tuscan ' villa ' ;
it is not the record of an idler.

IV Quaeris quemadmodum in Tuscis [1] diem aestate
disponam. Evigilo, cum libuit, plerumque circa horam
primam, saepe ante, tardius raro ; clausae fenestrae manent.
Cogito si quid in manibus [a] ; notarium voco et, die admisso,
quae formaveram dicto : abit rursusque revocatur rursusque
dimittitur.

Hora quarta vel quinta, ut dies suasit, in xystum me vel
crypto-porticum confero, reliqua meditor et dicto. Vehiculum ascendo ; ibi quoque idem quod ambulans aut
jacens. Paulum redormio, dein ambulo, mox orationem
graecam latinamve clare et intente, non tam vocis causa
quam stomachi,[2] lego. Iterum ambulo, ungor, exerceor,
lavor. [b] Cenanti [c] mihi, si cum uxore vel paucis, liber legitur :
post cenam comoedus [d] aut lyristes : mox cum meis ambulo,

[a] The ancients realised that in bed of a morning (with ' shutters
closed ') was a capital time for getting new ideas if you ' had any
writing on hand '.

[b] Like the Greeks, the Romans were fond of taking ' constitu-
tionals ', but they cared less about sport for sport's sake, regarding
exercise as a means of keeping fit, and whetting the appetite. The
exercise which Pliny took was probably a game called the ' Tri-
angle ', in which three players threw and caught a ball with their
left hands only. The players stripped and oiled themselves all
over, then after exercise entered first the Turkish bath, next the hot
bath and finally, after a cold plunge to close the pores of the skin,
had what remained of the oil scraped off with a metal instrumen
called a ' strigil '.

[c] Roman meals were as follows : breakfast or *jentaculum* at about
9 a.m., consisting of wine and bread with dried fruit, honey or
cheese ; lunch or *prandium* at noon, consisting of the cold remains
of the previous day's dinner : dinner or *cena* at about 4 p.m., the
one heavy meal of the day.

[d] A *comoedus* or ' comedian ' was an entertainer, usually one of
the host's own retinue, who gave recitations, no doubt with much
pantomimic gesture.

[1] ' at my Tuscan house '.   [2] ' digestion '.

quorum in numero sunt eruditi. Ita variis sermonibus vespera extenditur.

Nonnumquam ex hoc ordine aliqua mutantur. Interveniunt amici ex proximis oppidis partemque diei ad se trahunt. Venor aliquando, sed non sine pugillaribus,[3] ut, quamvis nihil ceperim, nonnihil referam. Datur et colonis, ut videtur ipsis, non satis temporis, quorum mihi agrestes querellae litteras nostras et haec urbana opera commendant.[4] [IX 36]

[3] 'note-book' (see VII, note a).
[4] 'their grumbles make me appreciate my literary work and such civilised occupations'.

PLINY THE WRITER

THERE were few idle moments in Pliny's 'Tuscan' day; but he himself regarded it almost as a holiday, a welcome break in the irksome routine of town-life. For, like his uncle, he was nearly always busy with a variety of public duties and interests. He worked hard as a lawyer. He was one of the officials in charge of the State Treasury. He served as 'curator of the Tiber-banks and city-sewers'. He held in turn the chief offices of state culminating in the consulship. He was a member of the Senate, and even sat on the Emperor's Privy Council—a very high distinction. Finally he was sent abroad to Bithynia in Asia Minor as special commissioner.

But, conscientiously as Pliny shouldered these responsibilities, his heart was not in them. His real interest (as the above letter shows) was in writing. Even during his lifetime —to his own great delight—his publications were bought and read as far away as Lyons in Southern Gaul; and it was as an author that he would have wished to go down to posterity. Among his friends he counted many famous writers. He was allowed to correct the first draft of Tacitus' histories. He was intimate with Suetonius, the biographer of the early Emperors. Martial wrote a poem in his honour. From his letters we learn how he and his friends attended one another's recitations of their works and sent one another copies of anything they published. Literature was, in short, the ruling passion of the circle in which he moved. Even the letters themselves were highly polished literary compositions. Pliny wrote them with elaborate care. He intended them for publication; and indeed they bear the mark of it.

Let us take a sample—a commonplace little letter, but obviously written with self-conscious attention to style.

V C. PLINIUS CALPURNIO MACRO SUO S.[a]

Bene est mihi, quia tibi bene est. Habes uxorem tecum, habes filium ; frueris mari, fontibus, agro, villa amoenissima. Neque enim dubito esse amoenissimam in qua se composuerat homo felicior. Ego in Tuscis et venor et studeo, quae interdum alternis, interdum simul facio ; nec tamen adhuc possum pronuntiare utrum sit difficilius capere aliquid an scribere. Vale. [b] [V 18]

[a] Roman letters began like the letter quoted in the Acts of the Apostles, ' Claudius Lysias unto the most excellent governor Felix greeting '. The Latin for ' greeting ' was sometimes *salutem dat* (abbreviated to S.D.), sometimes *salutem plurimam dat* (S.P.D.), sometimes, for short, simply *salutem* (S.).

[b] Letters closed always with ' farewell '.

¶. In order to appreciate an author's style it is well to enquire into the character of his education. Like most little Roman ' gentlemen ', Pliny must first have passed through a grammar school, where he would learn the rudiments of reading, writing and arithmetic, together with some training in music. Here such classical authors as Cicero, Livy, and Virgil would be studied and, in Greek, Homer and Demosthenes. Large passages were learnt by heart. At about fifteen he would pass on to a School of Rhetoric—an accomplishment then considered essential, since by long tradition public speaking and pleading in the Law Courts were very important elements in civic life. Pliny was a pupil of Quintilian, the leading Roman authority on style ; but all Roman oratory (we must remember) was ultimately based on the model of the Greeks, the first literary ' stylists '. With Pliny, as with most Latin authors, the effect of such training was an over-emphasis on style ; in other words, he thought almost more about the manner in which his ideas were expressed than about the ideas themselves. Even in his letters rhetorical tricks are frequent, and we may note one or two which are exemplified in the letter above :

A. Antithesis or contrast, e.g. in line 1 *mihi* contrasted with *tibi*, or in the last two lines *capere* with *scribere*.

B. Repetition, e.g. *habes* uxorem, *habes* filium.

Then again the authors of Pliny's day strove to be epigrammatic. Tacitus could cram more meaning into half a dozen words than any man who ever lived ; and Pliny admired Tacitus greatly. Hence he tends to omit (*a*) conjunctions between e.g. *mari, fontibus, agro* ; (*b*) verbs, e.g. in Piece XXXII *B*, l.13 . . . '*jam hora prima*' for '*jam hora prima erat*', as we might say ' Then a blare of trumpets ; and His Majesty appeared '. In the letters which follow, it will be worth while to note with some care these various devices of style.

In contrast to modern letters which usually contain a string of unconnected items, Pliny's letters nearly always deal with a single topic or episode. Sometimes, as in the following letter, this was an incident of which he had just heard. The ill-treatment of slaves was an ugly symptom of Roman brutality. Savage punishments such as beating, branding, and even crucifixion were all too common ; and under the Republic at any rate there was no legal redress or protection for the slave, who was simply regarded as his master's chattel. By Pliny's time things had begun to improve ; but many masters were still abominably cruel, particularly perhaps when they were self-made men, like the master of this story, himself the son of a slave. No wonder the victims of his brutality retaliated.

VI Rem atrocem Largius Macedo, superbus dominus et saevus, a servis suis passus est. Lavabatur in villa Formiana : repente eum servi circumsistunt : alius fauces invadit, alius os verberat ; alius pectus et ventrem contundit ; et cum exanimem putarent, abiciunt in fervens pavimentum, ut experirentur an viveret. Ille, sive quia non sentiebat, sive quia se non sentire simulabat, immobilis et extentus

fidem peractae mortis implevit.[1] Tum demum quasi aestu
solutus [2] effertur. Excipiunt servi fideliores : famulae cum
ululatu et clamore concurrunt. Ita et vocibus excitatus et
recreatus loci frigore, sublatis oculis agitatoque corpore
vivere se confitetur. Diffugiunt servi ; quorum magna pars
comprehensa est, ceteri requiruntur. Ipse, paucis diebus
aegre focilatus [3], non sine ultionis solacio [4] decessit. [III 14]

¶ Sometimes the incident is related simply in order to
illustrate a theory or a problem ; as in the following letter,
where the problem is the existence of ghosts.

VII Velim scire, phantasmata habere propriam figuram
putes an ex metu nostro imaginem vanam accipere.[1] . . .
Erat Athenis spatiosa et capax domus, sed infamis et pestilens.
Per silentium noctis sonus ferri et strepitus vinculorum
longius primo, deinde e proximo reddebantur [2] : mox
apparebat senex macie et squalore confectus,[3] promissa
barba, horrenti capillo : cruribus compedes, manibus catenas
gerebat quatiebatque. Inde inhabitantibus tristes diraeque
noctes per metum vigilabantur [4] ; vigiliam morbus et,
crescente formidine, mors sequebatur. Deserta inde
domus, totaque illi monstro relicta : proscribebatur [5] tamen,
seu quis emere, seu quis conducere vellet. Venit Athenas
philosophus Athenodorus, legit titulum, auditoque pretio
quia suspecta vilitas, percunctatus omnia docetur [6] ; ac
nihilo minus, immo tanto magis conducit.

---

[1] ' completed their conviction of his death's being an accom-
plished fact '.
[2] ' as though overcome by the heat '.
[3] ' nursed back to life '.
[4] ' not without the consolation of knowing himself avenged ',
i.e. by their execution.
VII [1] ' whether you think it is our own fears which give ghosts
their insubstantial shape '.
[2] ' echoed from nearby '.
[3] ' in the last stages of emaciation or squalor '.
[4] ' nights were rendered wakeful for the inmates '.
[5] ' advertised '.   [6] ' when he enquired, he was told all '.

Ubi coepit advesperascere, poscit pugillares,[a] stilum,
lumen : suos omnes in interiora dimittit, ipse ad scribendum
animum intendit. Initio silentium noctis : dein concuti
ferrum, vincula moveri. Ille non tollere oculos, non remit-
tere stilum. Tum crebescere fragor, adventare, et jam in
limine, jam intra limen audiri. Respicit, videt narratam
sibi effigiem. Stabat innuebatque digito. Hic contra ut
paulum exspectaret, manu significat rursusque ceris et stilo
incumbit. Illa scribentis capiti catenis insonabat. Respicit
rursus innuentem,[7] nec moratus tollit lumen et sequitur.
Ibat illa lento gradu, quasi gravis vinculis : postquam
deflexit in aream, repente dilapsa deserit comitem. Desertus,
herbas et folia concerpta signum loco ponit. Postero die
adit magistratus, monet ut illum locum effodi jubeant.
Inveniuntur ossa inserta catenis et implicita ; quae collecta
publice sepeliuntur. Domus postea rite conditis manibus
caruit.[8] [VII 27]

[a] For note-books the Romans used *pugillares* (derived from
pugnus =fist). These were folding-tablets of wood, rather like a
couple of slates, the inside face of which was covered with wax.
On the wax the writing was traced with a metal instrument called a
stilus ; when done with, the writing could be smoothed out and the
same wax used again and again.

❡ Sometimes a letter is nothing more than an excuse for
telling a good story ; as, for instance, this remarkable tale
which Pliny says he heard told at a dinner-party. In point of
fact he could have read it in his uncle's *Natural History* ;
perhaps he had !

VIII Est in Africa Hipponensis colonia,[a] mari proxima :
adjacet navigabile stagnum. Omnis hic aetas [1] piscandi,
navigandi atque etiam natandi studio tenetur, maxime
pueri. His gloria altissime provehi : victor ille, qui longis-

[7] ' looked back and saw it beckoning once more '.
[8] ' After that the house was free from the ghost (*mānes* plural)
which had thus been duly laid '.
VIII [1] ' men of all ages '.

sime **ut** litus ita simul natantes reliquit.[2] Hoc certamine puer quidam audentior ceteris in ulteriora tendebat. Delphinus occurrit et nunc praecedere puerum, nunc sequi, nunc circumire, postremo subire trepidantemque perferre in altum, mox flectit ad litus redditque terrae.[3] Serpit per coloniam fama : concurrere omnes, ipsum puerum aspicere, interrogare. Postero die obsident litus, prospectant mare. Delphinus rursus ad puerum. Fugit ille cum ceteris. Delphinus, quasi revocet, exsilit, mergitur, variosque orbes implicat expeditque.[4] Crescit audacia experimento. Puer adnatat, insilit tergo, fertur referturque, agnosci se et amari putat, amat ipse ; neuter timet, neuter timetur ; hujus fiducia, mansuetudo illius augetur. Incredibile [5] delphinum in terram quoque extrahi, harenisque siccatum, ubi incaluisset, in mare revolvi. Confluebant omnes ad spectaculum magistratus, quorum adventu respublica novis sumptibus atterebatur. [b] Postremo locus ipse quietem suam perdebat. Placuit occulte interfici ad quod coibatur.[6] [IX 33]

[a] A *colonia* was a town enjoying special privileges of self-government.

[b] Roman officials, visiting the town, had to be entertained at the town's expense.

[2] ' leaves furthest behind him both shore and comrades alike '.

[3] ' returns the boy to land '.

[4] ' performs evolutions ' (lit. ties and unties circles).

[5] sc. *est*.

[6] ' it was decided that the animal which drew such crowds (lit. to which it was come together) should be slaughtered '.

PLINY'S PUBLIC CAREER

THROUGHOUT her history Rome was essentially a militarist state. She had won her Empire through the superiority of her citizen-soldiers ; and she was now compelled to hold it against barbarian enemies by keeping large bodies of troops in her frontier provinces. The legions, it is true, were now drawn less and less from the population of Italy ; but the old tradition that a man should serve his country in a military capacity was still strong among the aristocracy ; and the first step for a young aspirant to a public career was almost invariably a commission in the army. Six subalterns or *tribuni militum* were apportioned to each legion. As the high command lay in the hands of a *legatus* or brigadier, and as discipline both in the field and in camp was maintained by non-commissioned sergeants or *centuriones*, there was not really much for these young gentlemen to do. They acted as orderly officers and superintended the commissariat. Pliny served in this capacity with a legion stationed in Syria. That eastern province, full of the riff-raff of the Levant, must have placed many temptations in the way of young subalterns, and he complains that the discipline was lax ; but he for his part was glad to find time to attend the lectures of professors of philosophy. In later life we know that his physique was none too good. He was thin and easily tired. Whether it was on this account or because he was clever at figures, the provincial governor (*legatus consularis*) had him seconded for special clerical work. During his year of service he made many friends ; and it was for one of these that he wrote the following letter of recommendation.

IX Claudius Pollio amari a te cupit, dignus hoc ipso, quod cupit,[1] deinde quod ipse te diligit. Vir rectus, integer, quietus ac paene ultra modum verecundus. Hunc, cum simul militaremus, ego non solum ut commilito inspexi.[2] Praeerat alae militari ; ego jussus a legato consulari rationes alarum et cohortium *a* excutere, ut quorumdam foedam avaritiam et neglegentiam, parem ita hujus summam integritatem, sollicitam diligentiam inveni.[3] Postea promotus ad amplissi-mas procurationes *b* nulla occasione corruptus ab insito abstinentiae amore deflexit ; numquam secundis rebus intumuit [4] ; numquam officiorum varietate continuam laudem humanitatis infregit [5] ; eademque firmitate animi laboribus suffecit, qua nunc otium patitur.

Hunc hominem adpetentissimum tui (mihi crede) com-plectere, immo et invita ac sic ama, tamquam gratiam referas.[6] [VII 31]

a An *ala* was a troop of cavalry. A ' cohort' was sometimes used of a sub-division of a legion ; here it refers to a body of auxiliary troops exclusively recruited from the provinces.

b *Procuratio* means a post in the provincial civil service, in which the temptations and opportunities of graft were many.

¶ Even before he went to the East for his year's military service, Pliny had begun his career at the bar. In this he was following the example of most prominent men both in his own and in earlier days. The fact is that there were not many professions open to the Roman ' gentleman '. It was an old tradition that they were debarred from taking any direct part in commerce or manufacture, though they often invested money in such undertakings. Medicine, architecture, and the arts generally, were left to Greeks and freedmen, and consequently were held in contempt. There remained for

[1] ' worthy for this very reason that he . . .'
[2] ' I got to know him not merely as a fellow officer (but also as a friend) '.
[3] ' as I found avarice, so too I found . . .'
[4] ' puffed up '.
[5] ' broke his record of honourable conduct '.
[6] ' repay a favour '.

the ' gentleman ' three possible careers—soldiering, administrative posts in Italy or the provinces, and pleading at the bar—that is, speaking in court on behalf of someone engaged in a law-suit.

The Romans were interested in legal proceedings to a degree which no other people has ever equalled. In part perhaps this was due to their temperament, for they were a pugnacious, self-assertive race, and enjoyed standing up for their rights. But in part too it was due to a desire to see justice done. Pleading at the bar was regarded as the ' noblest ' of professions, and it was even considered improper for an advocate to take a fee from his client, though presents were certainly offered and accepted at the close of the trial.

At Rome there were courts of various types, and the field covered by the cases which came before them was very wide. Besides criminal actions for theft, murder, and so forth, there were innumerable disputes about property, the sale of lands, houses, etc. There were suits about breach of commercial contracts—very numerous in days when Roman traders found their way into every corner of the Empire. Last, but not least, there were cases concerning inheritance, in which wills were contested by rival claimants or in which it was suspected that forgery had been committed. Inheritance cases normally came before the Court of the Centumviri or Hundred Men, and it was in this court that Pliny himself practised. By his day their number had been raised to 180, and they were usually divided into four separate courts. These ' judges ' (*judices*) sat in the Basilica Julia, a large hall built by Julius Caesar at the west end of the Forum. They were directed by a Chief Justice or *praetor* annually elected ; and the principles on which justice was to be dispensed rested largely with him. On entering office he issued an edict, defining what in his opinion those principles were. Usually he was content simply to reaffirm the pronouncement made by his predecessors, but a conscientious or enterprising praetor might add some fresh ruling, either because he found some point over which the laws

c

clashed with each other, or because new circumstances required a new treatment, or simply because (as in the following letter) he had raked up some *senatus consultum* or resolution of the Senate, which had been disregarded. Thus legal principles were handed down from one generation to another, each generation simplifying, elaborating or readjusting at need, and by this age-long process that great body of Roman Law, which has meant so much to European civilisation, was slowly but surely formulated.

In the following letter Pliny tells of the stir caused in Rome when a certain Licinius Nepos, the praetor directing the criminal courts, issued a new clause in his edict, and how the praetor who directed the Centumviral Court was in doubt whether he should do the same.

X Descenderam in basilicam Juliam. Sedebant judices, obversabantur [1] advocati ; silentium longum ; tandem a praetore nuntius ' dimittuntur centumviri '. Causa dilationis [2] Nepos praetor, qui proposuerat breve edictum. Suberat edicto senatus consultum hoc : OMNES QUI QUID NEGOTII HABERENT, JURARE JUBEBANTUR NIHIL SE OB ADVOCATIONEM CUIQUAM DEDISSE, PROMISISSE. Hoc facto Nepotis commotus praetor, qui centumviralibus praesidebat, deliberaturus an sequeretur exemplum, inopinatum nobis otium dedit.

Interim tota civitate Nepotis edictum carpitur,[3] laudatur. Multi : ' Invenimus, qui curva corrigeret.[4] Quid? Ante hunc praetores non fuerunt? Quis autem hic est, qui emendet publicos mores? ' Alii contra : ' Rectissime fecit ; initurus magistratum senatus consulta legit, reprimit foedissimas pactiones,[5] rem pulcherrimam turpissime venire non patitur.' [V 9]

❡ The Romans were nothing if not public-spirited. Under the Republic it had been almost a matter of course for men of

---

[1] ' were in their places '.   [2] ' postponement '.   [3] ' criticised '.
[4] ' put crooked things straight '.   [5] ' bargains '

good family to take public office ; and even in Pliny's day,
when all real political power was vested in the Emperor,
there was still no lack of candidates. The method of
election had by now become a mere formality. There was
no genuine freedom of choice. The Senate were presented
with a list of names, selected or approved by the Emperor,
and then voted upon them ; the public were only allowed to
attend the declaration of the result and cheer the successful
candidates—a great change from the days when the citizens
had themselves been the voters.

Pliny passed, step by step, through the usual succession
of magistracies. Some involved heavy administrative duties ;
others were more or less ornamental. None were paid.
The rate of promotion was regulated by a schedule of age-
limits. At twenty-eight he became one of the *quaestors* or
under-secretaries to the Treasury—the lowest rung of the
ladder. At thirty he was *tribune*—no longer a post of importance. After another two years he was a *praetor* or judge and
as such took part in the trial of a notorious provincial governor
named Baebius. Meanwhile the financial abilities he had
shown as a quaestor had attracted attention ; and as a result
the Emperor appointed him at thirty-seven to be chief
controller of the Treasury—a post which, he complains,
kept him chained to his ' stool ', making up accounts, jotting
comments on official papers, and writing innumerable ' most
unliterary ' letters.

Finally in his fortieth year he attained the consulship.
This office now enjoyed but a shadow of its glory in former
days, when its holder had been for a whole year chief minister
of the State and commander-in-chief of the armies. Now,
its tenure only lasted a couple of months, and its functions
were practically confined to presiding over the occasional
meetings of the Senate. Amongst other duties it fell to
Pliny's lot to return formal thanks to the Emperor after his
election. In his speech he told how Trajan, after being
adopted by Nerva, had on Nerva's death been acclaimed
Emperor in his absence, and how finally a year later he had

returned to Rome from the Rhine frontier. The extract
given here describes this triumphant return.

XI Jam te civium desideria [1] revocabant, amoremque
castrorum superabat caritas patriae.[2] Qui dies ille, quo
exspectatus desideratusque urbem tuam ingressus es !
Priores [3] invehi et importari solebant, non, dico, quadrijugo
curru et albentibus equis,[a] sed humeris hominum. Tu
sola corporis proceritate [4] elatior aliis et excelsior. Ergo
non aetas quemquam, non valetudo, non sexus retardavit
quominus oculos insolito spectaculo impleret. Te parvuli [5]
noscere, ostentare juvenes, mirari senes. Aegri quoque,
neglecto medentium imperio, ad conspectum tui, quasi ad
salutem sanitatemque, prorepere.[6] Videres referta [7] tecta,
oppletas undique vias angustumque tramitem [8] relictum
tibi : alacrem hinc atque inde populum, ubique par gaudium
paremque clamorem. Ubi vero coepisti Capitolium [a]
ascendere, quam laeta omnibus adoptionis tuae recordatio !
Quam peculiare [9] gaudium eorum qui te primi eodem loco
salutaverant imperatorem ! [Pan. XX–XXIII]

[a] When a victorious general returned from the wars he was
usually accorded a triumphal entry, proceeding in a car drawn by
white horses along the Sacred Way, which led through the Forum,
and then mounting the steps up to the Capitol or Citadel, where he
gave thanks in the temple of Jupiter.

℃. The quaestorship automatically admitted its holder to the
Senate ; so at a comparatively early age Pliny became a life-
member of that historic body. But, great as was its prestige,
the powers of the Senate had in the main been shorn away.
Once it had ruled the State. Now in passing its resolutions
or *senatus consulta* it was merely the mouthpiece of the

[1] ' the people's longing for you '.
[2] ' your affection for your country '.　　[3] sc. *imperatores*.
[4] ' tallness of stature '.
[5] diminutive of *parvus*, ' tiny children '.
[6] ' crept out as though to (regain) their safety and health '.
[7] ' crowded '.　　　　[8] ' path '.　　　　[9] ' special '.

Emperor's will. Its most active function was as a Supreme Court of Justice, and the following extract will give some idea of its procedure. Its sessions were usually held in the Senate-house or *curia* at the west end of the Forum opposite the Basilica Julia. One of the consuls presided. First came speeches for the prosecution and defence. Then each member, beginning with the ex-consuls or *consulares*, was invited to express his opinion (*censere*). Finally there was a ' division ' (*discessio*) : the presiding consul moved that one of the foregoing proposals (*sententiae*) should be adopted ; and those who agreed flocked to his side of the floor.

So far as formalities were concerned every attempt was made to preserve the dignity of the past, and Pliny's pride is evident when the Senate lived up to its reputation. It did so on this occasion. For the provincial governor, who was ' in the dock ', applied in vain for a special court of jurors, which presumably would have been easier to bribe, and was condemned by the almost unanimous vote of the House. Elsewhere, however, Pliny admits with shocked shame that its behaviour was not always so respectable and that the voting-tablets, served out for use in elections, were sometimes scribbled with the most undignified jokes !

XII Solet esse gaudio tibi, si quid actum est in senatu dignum ordine illo. Accipe ergo quod per hos dies actum est, severitate exempli salubre,[1] rei magnitudine aeternum.[2]

Marius Priscus accusantibus Afris quibus pro consule praefuit, judices petiit. Ego et Cornelius Tacitus, adesse provincialibus jussi, existimavimus fidei nostrae convenire [3] notum senatui facere excessisse Priscum immanitate et saevitia crimina, quibus dari judices possent,[4] cum ob innocentes condemnandos, interficiendos etiam, pecunias accepisset. Magna contentio, magni utrimque clamores. Novissime consul designatus Julius Ferox, vir rectus et

---

[1] ' healthy ', ' salutary '.   [2] ' ever to be remembered '.
[3] ' that it was our duty '.
[4] ' passed the (limit of) charges suitable to a special court '.

sanctus, censuit evocandos quibus diceretur innocentium
poenas vendidisse ; quae sententia praevaluit.

Venerunt, qui adesse erant jussi, Vitellius Honoratus et
Flavius Marcianus ; ex quibus Honoratus trecentis milibus *a*
exilium equitis Romani *b* septemque amicorum ejus ultimam
poenam, Marcianus unius equitis Romani septingentis
milibus plura supplicia arguebatur emisse ; erat enim
fustibus [5] caesus, damnatus in metallum,[6] strangulatus in
carcere.

Dilata est res in proximum senatum ; cujus ipse conspectus
augustissimus fuit. Princeps praesidebat ; erat enim consul.
Imaginare quae sollicitudo nobis, quibus super tanta re
praesente Caesare dicendum erat. Equidem in senatu non
semel egi ; tunc me tamen omnia novo metu permovebant.
Animum collegi ; coepi dicere. Dixi horis paene quinque ;
nam XII clepsydris, *c* quas acceperam, sunt additae quattuor.
Caesar quidem mihi tantum studium, tantam etiam curam,
(nimium est enim dicere sollicitudinem) praestitit, ut
libertum meum post me stantem saepius admoneret voci
consulerem,[7] cum me vehementius putaret intendi quam
gracilitas [8] mea perpeti posset.

Postero die dixit pro Mario Salvius Liberalis, vir subtilis,
acer, disertus : in illa vero causa omnes artes suas protulit.
Respondit Cornelius Tacitus eloquentissime.

Cornutus Tertullus, consul designatus, vir egregius et
pro veritate firmissimus, censuit septingenta milia, quae
acceperat Marius, aerario [9] inferenda, Mario urbe Italiaque
interdicendum.[10] Adsenserunt omnes usque ad Pompeium
Collegam ; ille septingenta milia aerario inferenda, Marium
poenae, quam jam passus esset, censuit relinquendum.[11]
Erant in utraque sententia multi. Sed, cum fieret discessio,
qui sellis consulum adstiterant, in Cornuti sententiam ire

---

[5] ' clubs '.   [6] ' mine '.   [7] ' spare my voice '.
[8] ' thinness ', ' meagre frame '.
[9] ' Public Treasury '.   [10] ' ban of exile passed on '.
[11] ' should be left to the penalty (for extortion) to which he had
already been sentenced '.

coeperunt. Collega cum paucis relictus. Hic finis cognitionis
amplissimae. [II 11]

^a The handiest Roman coin was the silver *denarius* referred to in
the Gospels as a ' penny ', but in reality worth about 10d. This
was sub-divided into four *sestertii* worth 2½d. each, and the sester-
tius was the unit commonly used in reckoning large sums. Thus
1,000 sestertii would be worth roughly £10, though the purchasing
power of the sum was far greater in Roman times. Often, as above,
the genitive *sestertiorum* is omitted with the numeral *milibus*.

^b A Roman ' knight ' or *eques* was simply a man of the middle-
class (generally a man engaged in financial or commercial transac-
tions) whose property was valued above a certain high figure. In
early days, only the rich could provide a war-horse and so serve as
equites or cavalrymen.

^c *Clepsydra* is a Greek word for a water-clock, constructed on the
principle of the hour-glass containing sand. By means of it a
certain portion of time was allotted to each speaker.

¶ It had been the practice of previous emperors to summon
for occasional consultation a small body of prominent men.
The composition of this Privy Council varied with the
character of the emperor who chose them. Juvenal the
satirist wrote an amusing parody of what happened under
Domitian. A midnight summons brought the Councillors
out to the royal ' villa ' at Alba. There an urgent problem
had arisen. A huge mullet had been presented to the
Emperor and it was too large to go on a dish. Was it to be
divided in pieces? The views of the Councillors were
desired. They were a motley crew. One had himself been
a fishmonger in humbler days. Another, a wily old flatterer,
affected astonishment at the monster, turning to the right,
when unfortunately the fish was all the time on his left—for
he was as blind as a bat ! Finally a fat gourmet settled the
question—a special dish must be constructed for the occasion.

Trajan chose his councillors with more discrimination and
Pliny here describes how he himself was summoned for the
trial of some cases in which appeal had been made to ' Caesar's
judgment-seat '. It is interesting to note what comparatively
trivial matters the Emperor found time to attend to.

XIII Evocatus in consilium a Caesare nostro ad Centum Cellas (hoc loco nomen) maximam cepi voluptatem. Quid enim jucundius quam principis justitiam, gravitatem, comitatem inspicere? Fuerunt variae cognitiones. Dixit causam Claudius Ariston, princeps Ephesiorum, homo munificus et popularis. Inde invidia, et delator immissus.[1] Itaque absolutus est.

Sequenti die audita est Gallitta adulterii rea. Nupta haec et suam et mariti dignitatem centurionis amore maculaverat.[2] Maritus legato consulari, ille Caesari scripserat. Caesar, excussis probationibus,[3] centurionem exauctoravit[4] atque etiam relegavit. Damnata[5] et Juliae legis *a* poenis relicta est.

Adhibebamur cotidie cenae : erat modica, si principem cogitares.[6] Interdum acroamata[7] audiebamus, interdum jucundissimis sermonibus nox ducebatur. Summo die abeuntibus nobis xenia[8] sunt missa. [VI 31]

a A very strict marriage law passed by Augustus.

¶ It was the usual thing for a consul after his term of office at Rome to pass on to the governorship of a province, but Pliny was an exception, and it was not until some years later that Trajan pressed him to go out to Bithynia on a special mission.

Since the days of Alexander's conquest of the East, Greek culture had spread all over Asia Minor, and the Bithynians were thoroughly hellenised. Town-life had become the fashion—town-life with all its organised luxuries, public baths, theatres, gymnasiums, water-supply and the rest. The Roman governors did not as a rule interfere very much with

[1] ' hence his unpopularity and the setting of an informer against him '.

[2] ' besmirched her husband's rank by a love affair with a sergeant '.

[3] ' examined the evidence '.   [4] ' cashiered '.

[5] sc. *Gallitta* as subject of sentence.

[6] ' if you remember it was an Emperor's banquet '.

[7] ' entertainments '.   [8] ' parting presents '.

the self-government of such towns ; and the result was that
the irresponsible Bithynians had been grossly extravagant.
More had been spent on public comforts than the munici-
palities could afford and their finances had got into a sad
muddle. Pliny was sent out by the Emperor to supersede the
ordinary governor appointed by the Senate, and it was his
business, if possible, to set the muddle right.

For a man of his habits and tastes it cannot have been a
very congenial task to leave Italy and undertake the fatigues
of travel in a trying climate. In the following letters we may
read his somewhat querulous account of the journey and
Trajan's dignified but half-humorous replies. The Emperor
clearly thought his commissioner a trifle fussy about health.

XIV   *A.*   C. PLINIUS TRAJANO IMPERATORI

Quia confido, domine, ad curam tuam pertinere, nuntio
tibi me Ephesum cum omnibus meis navigasse. Quamvis
contrariis ventis retentus, nunc destino partim orariis [1]
navibus, partim vehiculis provinciam petere ; nam, sicut
itineri graves aestus, ita continuae navigationi etesiae
reluctantur.[2] [X 15]

B.   TRAJANUS PLINIO

Recte renuntiasti, mi Secunde carissime. Pertinet enim
ad animum meum, quali itinere in provinciam pervenias.
Prudenter autem constituis interim navibus, interim vehiculis
uti. [X 16]

C.   C. PLINIUS TRAJANO IMPERATORI

Sicut saluberrimam navigationem, domine, usque ad
Ephesum sum expertus, ita inde, postquam vehiculis iter
facere coepi, gravissimis aestibus atque etiam febriculis [1]

A. [1] ' coasting vessels '.
   [2] ' just as the heat impedes land-travel, so the Etesian (or seasonal)
winds impede continuous sailing '.
C. [1] ' little feverish attacks '.

vexatus, Pergami substiti.[2] Rursus, cum transissem in
orarias naviculas, contrariis ventis retentus, aliquanto tardius
quam speraveram—id est xv Kalendas Octobres [a]—
Bithyniam intravi. Non possum tamen de mora queri, cum
mihi contigerit natalem [3] tuum in provincia celebrare.
Nunc reipublicae Prusensium impendia excutio [4] : quod ex
ipso tractatu [5] magis ac magis necessarium intelligo. [X 17a]

[a] The Roman method of dating was as follows :
    In every month there were three fixed days :
    The Kalends, always the first of the month.
    The Nones, usually the fifth of the month.*
    The Ides, usually the thirteenth of the month.*
Other days were reckoned by counting *backwards* from these
(days at *both* ends being counted for purposes of subtraction). To
find the 15th day before the Kalends of October, start on October
1st, and counting back you will find that the 15th day is Septem-
ber 17th.

* In March, July, October and May, the Nones were the seventh,
the Ides the fifteenth day.

D. TRAJANUS PLINIO

Cuperem sine querela corpusculi tui [1] pervenire in Bithyniam potuisses.[2] Quo autem die pervenisses, cognovi,
Secunde carissime, litteris tuis. Provinciales, credo, pro-
spectum sibi [3] a me intelligent. Nam tu dabis operam ut
manifestum sit illis electum te esse, qui mei loco mittereris.
Rationes autem in primis tibi rerum publicarum excutiendae
sunt ; nam esse eas vexatas satis constat. [X 18]

¶. It is interesting to see what detailed reports of his mission
Pliny thought fit to send back to Trajan. He consults him
about the most trifling details ; and if every provincial

[2] ' halted '.   [3] ' birthday '.
[4] ' examine accounts '.
[5] ' from actually handling (the matter) '.
D. [1] ' complaints about your poor little body '.
[2] Late usage for *te potuisse*.
[3] ' I have consulted their interests ', sc. *esse*.

official gave his master so much trouble, the burden of the
Emperor's daily routine must have been almost intolerable.
For instance, Pliny poses the following questions in a whole
series of letters : ' May the folk of Prusa restore a dilapidated
bath-house at the town's expense? ' ' A half-finished
gymnasium at Nicomedia has been burnt down, should it be
rebuilt? ' ' Nicomedia has spent a small fortune on building
two aqueducts, both of which have been abandoned ; shall
I start them on a third? ' ' Is the jail to be guarded by
soldiers or public slaves? ' ' Two runaway slaves have been
found among the recruits ; should they be executed? '

Trajan's replies are admirable in their business-like grasp
of each problem. They waste no words and, going straight
to the heart of each matter, they indicate clearly the principles which he wishes to see followed.

At Nicomedia Pliny explains that precautions against fire
are needed and that for this purpose he wishes to organize
a guild or *collegium* of firemen (like the guilds sometimes
formed by craftsmen, smiths, carpenters and so forth). But
such guilds were little favoured by the authorities, who
viewed with alarm the formation of any secret society
(*hetaeria*) which might take a political trend and so promote
plotting and treason. It was this fear which made them so
suspicious of the early Christian Church ; and it led on this
occasion to Trajan's veto on the formation of even a firemen's
guild.

XV *A.* C. PLINIUS TRAJANO IMPERATORI

Cum diversam partem [1] provinciae circumirem, Nico-
mediae vastissimum incendium multas privatorum domos et
duo publica opera, quamquam via interjacente, absumpsit.
Est autem latius sparsum primum violentia venti, deinde
inertia hominum, quos satis constat otiosos et immobiles
tanti mali spectatores perstitisse ; et alioqui [2] nullus usquam

[1] ' a different district '.
[2] ' apart from that '.

in publico sipho,[3] nulla hama,[4] nullum denique instrumentum
ad incendia compescenda.[5] Et haec quidem, ut jam prae-
cepi, parabuntur. Tu, domine, dispice an instituendum
putes collegium fabrorum. Ego attendam ne quis nisi
faber recipiatur, neve jure concesso in aliud utatur[6] ; nec
erit difficile custodire[7] tam paucos. [X 33]

B. TRAJANUS PLINIO

Tibi quidem in mentem venit posse collegium fabrorum
apud Nicomedenses constitui. Sed meminerimus provinciam istam ejusmodi factionibus esse vexatam. Quodcumque nomen dederimus iis, qui in idem contracti fuerint,[1]
hetaeriae brevi[2] fient. Satius itaque est comparari ea, quae
ad coercendos ignes auxilio esse possint, admonerique
dominos praediorum[3] ut et ipsi incendia inhibeant ac, si res
poposcerit, accursu populi[4] ad hoc uti. [X 34]

[3] ' pump ', ' fire-engine '.   [4] ' fire-bucket '.   [5] ' extinguish '.
[6] ' use the privilege, if granted, for another purpose '.
[7] ' keep a watch on '.
B. [1] ' to those who are collected for a common purpose '.
[2] sc. *tempore.*   [3] ' owners of estates '.
[4] ' general summons of the townsfolk '.

TOWN LIFE

His public duties kept Pliny much at Rome; and despite his constant grumbling, town-life cannot have been wholly uncongenial to a man of his tastes. For one thing it kept him in touch with his numerous friends. Like most Romans, he was a sociable person; and we can see from his letters that dinner-parties, at which he was sometimes host, sometimes guest, played a large part in his life.

Dinner, as we have seen, started early; four in the afternoon was the usual hour. The dining-room or *tri-clinium*, as its very name indicates, contained three long couches, set round three sides of a central square table; on these the guests reclined at full length. The first course, called *gustatio*, consisted of hors d'œuvres—salads, shell-fish, eggs, etc., to whet the appetite. Then came the more solid dishes of meat, chicken, ham, and so forth, carried on trays or *fercula* (from *fero* = I carry). Finally the dessert, known as *mensae secundae*—cakes and dried fruits. Plenty of wine was served, more freely when eating was over; and then one of the party, as ' master of the feast ', decided in what proportions water and wine should be mixed (for the wine was a thick syrup and was seldom drunk neat). Diversion was provided by reciters, harpists, Spanish dancing-girls and even acrobats; and the fun was often kept up far into the night.

The dinner here described by Pliny seems to have been peculiarly vegetarian in character. But on the whole the Romans, especially the working class, were not such great meat eaters as we are.

XVI C. PLINIUS SEPTICIO CLARO SUO S.

Heus tu promittis ad cenam nec venis ! Paratae erant
lactucae [1] singulae, cochleae [2] ternae, ova [3] bina, alica [4] cum
mulso [5] et nive, olivae,[6] betacei,[7] cucurbitae,[8] bulbi,[9] alia
mille nec minus lauta. Audisses comoedos vel lectorem vel
lyristen vel (quae mea liberalitas) [10] omnes. At tu apud
nescioquem ostrea,[11] vulvas,[12] echinos,[13] Gaditanas [14] malu-
isti. Dabis poenas, non dico quas. Dure fecisti : invidisti,[15]
nescio an tibi, certe mihi, sed tamen et tibi. Quantum nos
lusissemus, risissemus, studuissemus ! Potes apparatius [16]
cenare apud multos, nusquam hilarius, simplicius, incautius.
In summa experire,[17] et nisi postea te aliis potius excusa-
veris,[18] mihi semper excusa. Vale. [I 15]

¶ Another type of social gathering to which Pliny and his
circle were much given, was the literary recitation to which
we have alluded above. At this period books circulated
pretty freely. Copies could be produced in large numbers
by slaves. There were plenty of booksellers ; and authors
often sent their own works as a present to friends—sometimes
an unwelcome present, as Martial makes clear :

> Cur non mitto meos tibi, Pontiliane, libellos?
> Ne mihi tu mittas, Pontiliane, tuos.

There was, however, no easy method of advertising a new
work and the recitations served this purpose. Public halls
were sometimes hired ; sometimes the *conversazione*
took place in the author's own home. Pliny himself was
assiduous in his attendance on these occasions, even when

[1] ' lettuces '.   [2] ' snails '.   [3] ' eggs '.   [4] ' spelt ' (porridge).
[5] ' mead ' (a drink).   [6] ' olives '.   [7] ' beet-roots '.
[8] ' gourds '.   [9] ' onions '.   [10] ' such is my generosity '.
[11] ' oysters '.   [12] ' haggis '.   [13] ' sea-urchins '.
[14] ' dancing-girls from Cadiz '.
[15] ' done me a bad turn ' (lit. stint).
[16] ' more luxuriously '.   [17] ' in short give me a trial '.
[18] ' get out of dining with other folk '.

(as sometimes happened) the recitation ran on over three days. But many people, he complains, were deplorably slack, slinking in when the performance was half through and leaving again before the end. Here is an amusing account of a misunderstanding that arose because a member of the audience happened to bear the same name as the man to whom the poem of the reciter was dedicated.

XVII Passennus Paulus, splendidus eques Romanus, scribit elegos.[1] Is cum recitaret, ita coepit dicere ' Prisce, jubes '. Ad hoc Iavolenus Priscus (aderat enim, ut Paulo amicissimus) ' ego vero non jubeo.' Cogita qui risus hominum, qui joci. Est Priscus dubiae sanitatis, interest tamen officiis,[2] adhibetur consiliis[3] ; quo magis, quod tunc fecit, et ridiculum et notabile fuit. Interim Paulo aliena deliratio[4] aliquantum frigoris attulit. Tam sollicite recitaturis providendum est non solum ut sint ipsi sani,[5] verum etiam ut sanos adhibeant. [VI 15]

¶ The Roman man of culture prided himself on his versatility. Martial tells of an individual who could write poetry, play the harp, recite, dance, sing and tell fortunes ; and we shall not be surprised to learn that Pliny tried his hand at poetry. At the age of fourteen he had written a drama in Greek ; in later life he published a book of light verse. Martial more than hints that the staid orator wrote poetry best when ' in his cups '.

To the Muse of Poetry

Tipsy maiden, mark the hour.
Knock not on the Scholar's door,
While Minerva, goddess grim,
Casts *her* mantle over him,

---

[1] ' elegiac poetry '.   [2] ' takes part in public life '.
[3] ' is admitted to legal consultations '.
[4] ' another man's lunacy '.
[5] poets were supposed to be on the verge of madness

> And in privacy he cons
> His ' Chancery ' orations
> (Which Posterity—who knows?—
> May rank as high as Cicero's).
> Wait, my lass, and let him be,
> Till the wine is flowing free
> And roses wreathe the scented brow.
> Now's the moment ;   Try him now !
> Men love ditties, while they dine,
> Even prudes—and even mine.

Pliny seems to have been delighted at the compliment to his poetry, but he admits he was a poor hand at reciting it. He arranged therefore to leave that to his secretary, but he here writes to a friend in great uncertainty.   How is he to behave during the entertainment—sit mum or, like some others, accompany the reciter in dumb show, gesticulate, posture, in short, (he adds with humorous exaggeration) dance ?

XVIII Explica aestum meum.[1]   Audio me male legere versus.   Cogito ergo recitaturus familiaribus amicis, experiri libertum meum non bene, sed melius lecturum, si non fuerit perturbatus [2] ; est enim tam novus lector quam ego poeta. Ipse nescio quid, illo legente, interim faciam—sedeam defixus et mutus, an (ut quidam) quae pronuntiabit, murmure, oculis, manu prosequar.   Sed puto me non minus male saltare quam legere. Iterum dicam, explica aestum meum vereque rescribe, num sit melius pessime legere quam ista [3] vel non facere—vel facere. [IX 34]

¶. Besides these *conversazioni* social etiquette made many other demands upon Pliny's time.   The Romans always attached great importance to duty-calls, and men of lower station were expected to put in an appearance pretty fre-

---

[1] ' solve my dilemma '   [2] ' nervous '.
[3] ' what others do '

quently at the houses of their superiors or patrons—usually
first thing in the morning. Pliny himself no doubt received
such tiresome attentions, and on his own part he dutifully
responded (as this letter will show) to the invitations or
demands of his friends. At one time it might be a ' coming-
of-age ' ceremony,*a* when a youth doffed the *toga praetexta*
(a garment the hem of which was ornamented by a broad
purple stripe and which was the mark of a minor) and
assumed the *toga virilis* or ordinary plain toga which was the
mark of a full-grown man. At another time it might be a
betrothal *b* or a wedding *c* ; or again he might be called in to
witness the signing of another man's will or to tender some
legal advice.

XIX Si quem interroges, ' hodie quid egisti? ' respondeat,
' officio togae virilis *a* interfui ; sponsalia *b* aut nuptias *c*
frequentavi ; ille me ad signandum testamentum, ille in
consilium rogavit.' Haec quo die [1] feceris, necessaria, eadem,
si cotidie fecisse te reputes, inania videntur. Tunc enim
subit recordatio [2] ' quot dies quam frigidis [3] rebus absumpsi !'
Quod evenit mihi, postquam in Laurentino meo aut lego
aliquid aut scribo aut etiam corpori vaco.[4] Nihil audio quod
audisse, nihil dico quod dixisse paeniteat : nemo apud me
quemquam sinistris sermonibus [5] carpit ; neminem ipse
reprehendo—nisi me, cum parum commode [6] scribo. Nulla
spe, nullo timore sollicitor, nullis rumoribus inquietor.
Mecum tantum et cum libellis [7] loquor. O rectam sinceram-
que vitam ! O dulce otium honestumque ac paene omni
negotio pulchrius ! Proinde tu quoque strepitum istum
inanemque discursum [8] relinque teque studiis vel otio trade.
[I 9]

a, b, c, see paragraph on this page.

[1] sc. *eodem die quo*.
[2] ' the recollection enters my mind '.
[3] ' futile '. [4] ' enjoy physical repose '. [5] ' malicious talk '.
[6] ' not aptly enough '. [7] ' my papers '.
[8] ' the noise and pointless bustle ' (of the town).

D

¶ An interest in other peoples' wills was perhaps unavoidable for a man of Pliny's profession ; but there were others who took a different and less healthy interest in their contents. Childless marriages were at this time very common ; and certain shameless adventurers used to curry favour (*captare*) with rich men and women who had no heirs in the hopes of ultimately receiving a legacy. In the next extract Pliny tells three stories about a particularly notorious *captator* called Regulus.

XX Assem para et accipe auream fabulam,[1] fabulas immo ; nam me priorum nova admonuit.[2] Verania graviter jacebat.[3] Ad hanc Regulus venit : proximus toro sedit : quo die, qua hora nata esset, interrogavit. Ubi audiit, componit vultum, intendit oculos, movet labra, agitat digitos, computat ; nihil : ut diu miseram exspectatione suspendit[4] : ' habes ', inquit, ' climactericum tempus,*a* sed evades.' Illa, ut in periculo credula,[5] poscit codicillos, legatum Regulo scribit ; mox ingravescit[6] : clamat moriens, ' O hominem perfidum ac plus etiam quam perjurum ! ' Facit hoc Regulus frequenter. Velleius Blaesus, ille locuples consularis, novissima valetudine[7] conflictabatur ; cupiebat mutare testamentum. Regulus, qui speraret aliquid ex novis tabulis, medicos hortari, rogare, quoquo modo spiritum homini prorogarent.[8] Postquam signatum est testamentum, vertit adlocutionem,[9] isdemque medicis : ' Quousque miserum cruciatis? Quid invidetis bonam mortem,[10] cui dare vitam non potestis? ' Moritur Blaesus, et, tamquam omnia audisset, Regulo ne tantulum quidem.[11] Sufficiunt duae fabulae an tertiam

[1] ' get ready your penny and hear a golden tale '.
[2] ' reminds me of '.   [3] ' was seriously ill '.
[4] ' keeps her on tenterhooks '.
[5] ' as her critical condition made her credulous '.
[6] ' grows worse '.
[7] ' his last illness ' (lit. ' health ', so ' ill health ').
[8] ' prolong by whatever means '. *hortari* and *rogare*, historic infinitives.
[9] ' changed his tone '.   [10] ' why grudge a happy release ? '
[11] ' not even a trifle ', sc. some word like *legavit*.

poscis? Aurelia, ornata femina, signatura testamentum sumpserat pulcherrimas tunicas. Regulus, cum venisset ad signandum, ' rogo ', inquit, ' has mihi leges? ' Aurelia ludere hominem putabat, ille serio instabat.[12] Coegit mulierem aperire tabulas ac sibi tunicas, quas erat induta, legare : observavit scribentem,[13] inspexit an scripsisset. Et Aurelia quidem vivit. [II 20]

^a *Climactericum* (from a Greek word *climax* =ladder) was a term used by astrologers or fortune tellers, denoting years which were multiples of the magic numbers 7 and 9. The practice of astrology was much in vogue among the superstitious Romans of this time. Even Emperors did not disdain the services of a private expert.

¶, The bad taste of Regulus was unhappily typical of one class in Roman society. Like him, there were many who had risen from obscure beginnings to considerable fortune. The ostentatious display and vulgar manners of such *parvenus* stood in striking contrast to the studied moderation and prim dignity of Pliny's own circle. The writer Petronius gives an extraordinary picture of a dinner-party given by a man of this type. When the guests arrive, their nails are manicured. Negroes bring wine in skins for them to wash their hands in. The surprise dish of the feast is a roast boar, from the flank of which, when carved, issues a flight of live thrushes. Finally, as a climax, a contrivance is let down from the roof bearing a bottle of scent for each member of the party.

Even more depressing to the educated man was the utter degeneracy of the masses. The population of the capital was no longer in the main Roman- or even Italian-born. Greeks ' on the make ' wormed their way into all skilled jobs, as architects, surveyors, doctors and so forth. Swarms of orientals were everywhere. ' The rivers of the East ', says Juvenal, ' have flowed into the Tiber.' Thousands of paupers had to be supported by the state or by rich patrons. Above

[12] ' insisted in all seriousness '.
[13] sc. *testamentum*.

all, this motley crowd required to be amused. Spectacular
entertainments were an important part of Roman civilisation.
Even in small provincial towns such as Silchester or Caerleon
in Britain, the building of an amphitheatre was an inevitable
consequence of the Roman conquest. In the capital itself there was, of course, the Colosseum, in which bloody
fights between gladiators were the rule, and in which, in
times of persecution, Christians were thrown to the lions.
There were also theatres, catering for a slightly healthier
taste. Finally there was the Circus Maximus or race course.
Chariot races, which took place there, were all the rage.
Four capitalist companies arranged for the teams, the drivers
of which wore a coloured favour (*pannus*), white, red, blue or
green. It was a dangerous sport, for fatal accidents through
collision were frequent as the four-horse teams raced round
the sharp corners. The excitement was further stimulated
by reckless betting. Everyone became the backer of one or
other colour (as of some favourite football team to-day) and
feeling ran high between the rival factions. Pliny himself,
as we might expect, was not amused.

XXI Omne hoc tempus inter pugillares ac libellos jucundis-
sima quiete transmisi. ' Quemadmodum ', inquis, ' in urbe
potuisti? ' Circenses erant, quo genere spectaculi ne levis-
sime quidem teneor.[1] Nihil novum, nihil varium, nihil quod
non semel spectasse sufficiat. Quo magis miror tot milia
virorum tam pueriliter cupere currentes equos, insistentes
curribus homines videre. Si tamen aut velocitate equorum
aut hominum arte traherentur,[2] esset ratio nonnulla [3] ; nunc
favent panno, pannum amant ; et, si in ipso cursu hic color
illuc, ille huc transferatur, studium favorque transibit, et
repente agitatores [4] illos, equos illos, quorum clamitant
nomina, relinquent. [IX 6]

[1] ' interested '.   [2] ' attracted '.   [3] ' some sense in it '.
[4] ' drivers '.

COUNTRY LIFE

THE stress, discomforts and even dangers of city life are vividly depicted by Juvenal in one of his Satires. It tells the story of a man who has packed up his belongings and is preparing to migrate to the neighbourhood of Naples, and he explains the various reasons which are driving him from Rome. First, the appalling condition of the houses. For lack of space all but the rich were compelled to live in huge blocks, called *insulae* or islands. These were jerry-built tenements often several storeys high. The walls with their gaping cracks threatened at any moment to collapse, and fires were frequent, for the construction was largely of timber. Next, the traffic in the crowded narrow streets—pedestrians jostling, pushing, elbowing their way ; rich men's sedans forcing a passage through the crowd, wagons loaded with timber, herds of cattle bellowing and the drovers loud with curses, slaves hurrying along with a portable stove. The lot of the foot-passenger was not to be envied. Tiles fell from the roofs ; broken crockery was flung from the windows ; and slop-pails were emptied on his unwary head. Lorries loaded with marble might at any instant upset their cargo and squash the poor man flat. At night things were even worse. There were no street lamps, and only the rich could afford an escort of slaves to light them home. Roisterers from a dinner-party reeled along dead drunk, and foot-pads lurked in dark corners ready to spring.

In the light of this description we can well understand why Pliny made his escape, when he could, to his ' villa ' by the sea. As there were of course no Sundays, there were no week-end breaks, but festivals were frequent, and these, like the Saturnalia, often lasted several days. In any case, as Pliny himself explains, he could leave Rome when the morning's business was over and arrive by carriage in time to have a good portion of the day at his disposal, for the distance was only 17 miles. His Tuscan mansion, on the other hand, was useful for the summer months, when at Rome the heat became unbearable, if not downright unhealthy. In the following letter he explains its charms to a friend who fears that Etruria may be unhealthy too. At first sight his description appears to reveal a genuine appreciation of natural scenery, but it is probable that the Tuscan landscape with its vineyards and trim fields made more appeal to him than the wilder mountains of the northern lakes. The truth is that the taste for wild country is a modern development. Even the poet Gray, when paying his first visit to the Lake District, pulled down the blinds of his carriage, because he could not endure the bleakness of the view.

XXII Amavi [1] curam et sollicitudinem tuam quod, cum audisses me aestate Tuscos meos petiturum, ne facerem, suasisti, dum putas insalubres.[2] Ut omnem pro me metum ponas, accipe temperiem caeli,[3] regionis situm, villae amoenitatem ; quae et tibi auditu et mihi relatu jucunda erunt.

Caelum est hieme frigidum et gelidum ; myrtos, oleas, quaeque alia adsiduo tepore laetantur, aspernatur [4] : laurum tamen patitur atque etiam nitidissimam profert.[5] Aestatis mira clementia, semper aër spiritu aliquo movetur, frequentius tamen auras quam ventos habet. Hinc senes multi : videas avos proavosque jam juvenum,[6] audias fabulas veteres sermonesque majorum ; cumque veneris illo, putes alio te saeculo natum.

[1] ' I am grateful for '.
[2] ' advised me not to do so as you think (my house) unhealthy '.
[3] ' the temperate character of the climate '.
[4] ' does not allow to grow ', lit. ' scorns '.
[5] ' produces a fine sort ' (of laurel).
[6] ' full-grown men '.

Regionis forma pulcherrima. Imaginare amphitheatrum immensum, et quale sola rerum natura possit effingere.[7] Lata et diffusa planities montibus cingitur ; montes summa sui parte procera nemora et antiqua habent. Frequens ibi et varia venatio.[8] Inde caeduae [9] silvae descendunt. Has inter, pingues colles planissimis campis fertilitate non cedunt, opimamque messem [10] percoquunt. Sub his per latus omne [11] vineae porriguntur. Prata inde campique—campi quos non nisi ingentes boves et fortissima aratra perfringunt (tantis glebis tenacissimum [12] solum) ; prata florida et gemmea [13] herbas teneras alunt ; cuncta enim perennibus rivis nutriuntur. Medios agros Tiberis secat, navium patiens omnesque fruges devehit in urbem. [V 6]

❦ Once out at his rural estate Pliny liked to play the country-gentleman, and he mentions more than once that he went out boar-hunting. According to the usual fashion, nets were set up in the forests, leading to a funnel-neck into which, when driven by a cordon of beaters, the boars would rush, and there be dispatched by the sportsmen awaiting them. Pliny's heart, however, was not in the hunt ; and he here tells us how he was careful to take not merely his bread-basket and flask, but also note-books and pencil wherewith to wile away the long wait.

XXIII Ridebis, et licet rideas. Ego apros tres et quidem [1] pulcherrimos cepi. ' Ipse? ' inquis. Ipse : non tamen ut [2] omnino ab inertia et quiete discederem. Ad retia [3] sedebam ;

[7] ' such as Nature alone could fashion '.
[8] ' plenty of hunting of various types '.
[9] ' ripe for felling '.   [10] ' first-rate harvest '
[11] ' the whole mountain-side '.
[12] ' of such clods is the heavy (lit. clinging) soil composed '.
[13] ' bejewelled ' (with flowers).
XXIII [1] ' in fact '.
[2] ' yet without altogether abandoning . . .' (lit. ' I took them in such a way that I did not abandon . . .').
[3] ' nets '.

erat in proximo non venabulum aut lancea,[4] sed stilus et
pugillares : meditabar aliquid enotabamque, ut, si manus
vacuas, plenas tamen ceras [5] reportarem. Non est quod [6]
contemnas hoc studendi genus ; mirum est ut animus
agitatione motuque corporis excitetur.[7] Jam undique silvae
et solitudo ipsumque illud silentium, quod venationi datur,
magna cogitationis incitamenta sunt. Proinde, cum vena-
bere, licebit auctore me [8] ut panarium [9] et lagunculam,[10]
sic pugillares feras : experieris non Dianam [a] magis montibus
quam Minervam inerrare. [I 6]

[a] *Diana* (or Artemis) was the goddess of hunting whereas
Minerva (or Athene) was the goddess of learning and the arts.

❡ Pliny was far too conscientious to neglect, even when in
his country retreat, the duties and responsibilities of his
position. For one thing he had his tenants to think of.
There had been a time when the owners of large estates
farmed them for their own profit through slave-labour
controlled by a bailiff ; but unwilling workers seldom prove
satisfactory, and by Pliny's day it had been found more
advantageous to let out the farms to tenants or *coloni*. These
were men of small resources easily crippled by a bad harvest
and apt to fall in arrears with their rent. Pliny complains
bitterly of their everlasting grumbling, but he was an indul-
gent landlord and often allowed remission of rent. Eventually
he found it wiser to fall back on a plan whereby he received
a proportion of the produce—it was fairer, he said, that he
should share in the risks of farming.

Even outside the boundaries of his own property Pliny
was a man of importance. Near his Tuscan house was a
place called ' Tifernum-on-Tiber ', and its inhabitants asked
him to be their *patronus*—a position which meant that, if
need be, he would act for them in court and in general would

[4] ' hunting-spear or lance '.   [5] ' wax-tablets '.
[6] ' there is no reason why . . .'   [7] ' enlivened '.
[8] ' you may, on my advice . . .'
[9] ' bread-basket '.   [10] ' flask '.

look after their interests. We should call him the ' squire '
of the place, and he lived up to the part by building it a
Temple out of his own pocket. In the following letter to his
wife's grandfather, he announces his intention of attending
its dedication and giving the good folk a dinner.

XXIV C. PLINIUS FABATO PROSOCERO SUO S.

Cupis post longum tempus neptem tuam meque videre.
Gratum est utrique nostrum, quod cupis ; nam nos incredi-
bili desiderio vestri tenemur atque adeo jam sarcinulas
alligamus.[1] Erit una, sed brevis mora.[2] Deflectemus in
Tuscos, non ut agros remque familiarem oculis subiciamus
(id enim postponi potest) sed ut fungamur necessario
officio. Oppidum est praediis nostris vicinum (nomen
Tifernum Tiberinum), quod me, paene adhuc puerum,
patronum cooptavit.[3] Adventus meos celebrat, profection-
ibus angitur, honoribus gaudet. In hoc [4] ut referrem
gratiam, templum pecunia mea exstruxi, cujus dedicationem
differre longius irreligiosum est. Erimus ergo ibi dedica-
tionis die, quem epulo celebrare constitui. Subsistemus
fortasse et sequenti [5] ; sed tanto magis viam ipsam cor-
ripiemus.[6] Contingat [7] modo te filiamque tuam fortes
invenire ! nam hilares certum est,[8] si nos incolumes receper-
itis. Vale. [IV 1]

¶ Pliny also showed his public spirit in other and more
practical ways. To Como, his beloved birthplace, he gave
a public library ; he left a bequest for the building of baths ;
he gave a large sum for the support of boys and girls of poor
families ; and, as the next extract will show, he gave a splendid
lead for the provision of what we should call a High School.

Under the Roman Empire education was remarkably
widespread. In a little Portuguese mining-village an in-

[1] ' strapping up our baggage '. [2] ' one cause of delay '.
[3] ' elected as patron '. [4] sc. *oppido*. [5] sc. *die*.
[6] ' hasten our journey ', lit. ' devour the road '.
[7] ' may it be our good fortune '. [8] sc. *vos fore.*

scription which has been unearthed records that there was a local schoolmaster. In Britain, within a generation or so of its conquest, Agricola, Tacitus' father-in-law, did his best to encourage the learning of Latin ; and at Silchester in Hampshire there has been discovered a tile, on which the teacher at the end of a writing-lesson had scrawled a line from Virgil's *Aeneid*. Como, it goes without saying, must have possessed a grammar-school, but there was no ' school of rhetoric ' nearer than Milan, some twenty-five miles away ; and the more promising lads, who wished to carry their studies beyond the rudiments, had to go there and board away from home. In those days, of course, the State did not organise or finance education, any more than it did in England until the second half of the last century. The setting up of a school was therefore a private enterprise on the part of a teacher, unless (as at Como) the leading men of the place clubbed together to hire one. In this letter, which is addressed to Tacitus, Pliny asks his learned friend to select a teacher or two from among his many admirers ; it was his wish, however, that the parents themselves should make the final choice.

XXV Proxime, cum in patria mea fui, venit ad me salutandum municipis mei filius praetextatus.[1] Huic ego, ' studes? ' inquam. Respondit ' etiam '.[2] ' Ubi? ' ' Mediolani.' ' Cur non hic? ' et pater (ipse enim adduxerat puerum) ' quia nullos hic praeceptores habemus.' ' Quare nullos? nam vehementer intererat vestra qui patres estis ' (et opportune complures patres audiebant) ' liberos vestros hic potissimum discere. Ubi enim aut jucundius morarentur quam in patria, aut pudicius continerentur [3] quam sub oculis parentum, aut minore sumptu quam domi? Quantulum est,[4] collata pecunia, conducere praeceptores ; quodque nunc in habitationes, in viatica, in ea quae peregre emuntur,

---

[1] see p. 49.   [2] ' yes '.
[3] ' more decently controlled ', i.e. kept under better discipline.
[4] ' how small a matter it is '.

impenditis, adicere mercedibus.[5]   Atque adeo [6] ego, qui
nondum liberos habeo, paratus sum tertiam partem ejus,
quod conferre vobis placebit, dare.   Proinde consentite,
conspirate, majoremque animum ex meo sumite ; qui
cupio esse quam plurimum, quod debeam conferre.   Nihil
honestius praestare liberis vestris, nihil gratius patriae
potestis.' [IV 13]

  [5] ' to add to the teachers' salaries what you spend on board,
journey money and the things which are bought away from home
(lit. ' abroad ') '.
  [6] what is more '.

PHILOSOPHY AND CHARACTER

FROM the foregoing extracts we have learnt a good deal about Pliny's interests and occupations. It is time perhaps to look deeper and to sum up his character and consider his attitude towards life as a whole.

The Romans of the Imperial epoch were under few illusions. To them life with its worries and responsibilities, disappointments and tragedies, was a somewhat grim business ; and any thinking man was bound sooner or later to make up his mind how to face it. Religion helped him scarcely at all. The worship of the pagan gods had become a mere formality—a round of ceremonials which had no more spiritual significance than the singing of ' God Save the King ' (which after all is a hymn) at the beginning or end of a concert. The answer to the problem of life was therefore to be sought in philosophy. At this time there were two schools of philosophic thought. Each attempted, though in a quite different way, to define what constituted happiness. On the one side were the Epicureans—the followers of the Greek thinker Epicurus who had lived about the time of Alexander the Great. These Epicureans were what we should call ' escapists '. Their answer to the problem was briefly this : ' Keep clear of all responsibility and worry, retire into seclusion preferably in the country, and there enjoy the society of friends and books untroubled by the storm and stress of the great world's feverish life.' Some Romans, it is true, being shallow or vicious, sought to escape from life's troubles through sheer dissipation. ' Let us eat, drink and be merry ; for to-morrow we die.' But many held more closely to Epicurus' more refined definition of happiness, and their ideas were well summed up in a poem written by Pliny's friend Martial (x. 47).

XXVI Vitam quae faciant beatiorem,
jucundissime Martialis, haec sunt :
res non parta labore, sed relicta ;
non ingratus ager, focus perennis ;
lis numquam, toga rara, mens quieta ;
vires ingenuae, salubre corpus ,
prudens simplicitas, pares amici ;
convictus facilis, sine arte mensa ;
nox non ebria, sed soluta curis ;
somnus qui faciat breves tenebras ;
quod sis, esse velis nihilque malis ;
summum nec metuas diem nec optes.[1]

[1] Translation on p. 75.

℃, The rival philosophic creed was that of the ' Stoics '.
These took their name from the ' stoa ' or portico at Athens
in which its earliest professors taught. For them the solution
of the problem of life was to be found not by running away
from its difficulties, but by meeting them. ' Set your face ',
they said, ' unflinchingly ; do your duty ; play your part by
the society in which you are placed. Happiness is an inner
condition of the mind ; you must be independent, rise super-
ior to circumstances and find satisfaction in your victory over
them, " master of your fate and captain of your soul ".'
Whoever lives his life in such a way, is the perfect man—the
true, though uncrowned, ' King '. In the following poem
Seneca, the scholar-statesman of Nero's reign, summed
up this ideal of moral ' Kingship '. (*Thyestes*, 344 *et seq.*)

XXVII Regem non faciunt opes,
non vestis Tyriae color,
non frontis nota regiae,
non auro nitidae fores.
Rex est qui posuit metus
et diri mala pectoris ;
quem non ambitio impotens,
et numquam stabilis favor

vulgi praecipitis movet ;
quem non concutiet cadens
obliqui via fulminis,
non eurus rapiens mare,
aut saevo rabidus freto
ventosi tumor Hadriae :
quem non lancea militis,
non strictus domuit chalybs,
qui tuto positus loco
infra se videt omnia,
occurritque suo libens
fato, nec queritur mori.
Rex est qui metuit nihil.
Rex est qui cupiit nihil.
Hoc regnum sibi quisque dat.[1]

[1] Translation on p. 76.

℄ Pliny himself, like many other Romans, was much influenced by the Stoic creed. When a young subaltern in Syria, he attended the lecture of Stoic philosophers, and in one letter he describes a certain Euphrates, who had migrated from Syria to Rome and with whom he maintained a close friendship. He was a tall, handsome man with long hair and flowing beard who did not (like the strictest Stoics) affect an unkempt appearance and coarse clothes, yet was none the less an unsparing critic of slack ways or vicious habits. Under the early Emperors the uncompromising independence of many Stoics had got them into trouble. Some went to the length of actual treason. Paetus Thrasea (as is told in the following letter) had joined in an attempt to overthrow the Emperor Claudius and to restore political liberty to Rome. The unflinching courage with which this man, and still more his wife Arria, had met their fate, made a deep impression. Men regarded them as martyrs in a noble cause.

XXVIII Scribonianus arma in Illyrico contra Claudium moverat [1] ; fuerat Paetus in partibus [2] et occiso Scriboniano

[1] 'raised a revolt'. [2] 'on Scribonianus' side '.

Romam trahebatur. Erat ascensurus navem : Arria milites orabat ut simul imponeretur. ' Nempe enim ', inquit, ' daturi estis consulari viro servulos aliquos, quorum e manu cibum capiat, a quibus vestiatur, a quibus calcietur [3] : omnia sola praestabo.' Non impetravit : conduxit piscatoriam naviculam ingensque navigium minimo [4] secuta est. *Non multo post, cum mortem mariti certam praevideret, mori una destinavit.* Quin etiam, cum Thrasea, gener ejus, deprecaretur ne mori pergeret [5] interque alia dixisset, ' vis ergo filiam tuam, si mihi pereundum fuerit, mori mecum? ' respondit ' si tam diu tantaque concordia vixerit tecum, quam ego cum Paeto, volo.' Auxerat hoc responso curam suorum : attentius custodiebatur ; sensit et ' nihil agitis ' inquit : ' potestis enim efficere, ut male moriar ; ut non moriar, non potestis.' Dum haec dicit, exsiluit cathedra, adversoque parieti caput ingenti impetu impegit.[6] Focilata,[7] ' dixeram ', inquit, ' vobis, inventuram me quamlibet duram ad mortem viam,[8] si vos facilem negassetis.' *Neque hoc mortis pulcherrimae consilium reliquit ; quod mox manifestum fuit. Condemnatur Paetus ; sed datur ei facultas eligendi quo mortis genere malit perire. Tum repente Arria ferrum stringere, perfodere pectus, extrahere pugionem,[9] porrigere marito, addere vocem immortalem ac paene divinam* ' Paete, non dolet '.[10] [III 16]

Note.—The sentences in *italics* are not in Pliny and the position of the last sentence has been changed.

¶, In his own life Pliny was clearly not a consistent adherent of either the Stoic or the Epicurean creed. When engaged on affairs of state, he was a Stoic, sticking grimly to his duty and priding himself on it. But he does not conceal the fact that he longed for his intervals of leisurely country life and

---

[3] ' have his shoes put on '.   [4] sc. *navigio.*
[5] ' tried to dissuade her from going to the length of suicide '.
[6] ' dashed her head against the wall opposite '.
[7] ' nursed back to life '.
[8] ' a means to suicide however difficult you make it '.
[9] ' dagger '.   [10] ' it does not hurt '.

looked forward to the day when age would justify him in retiring altogether from public affairs and leading the life of the Epicurean recluse. The truth is that he was not a deep thinker, but simply a good man striving to live up to the best ideals of his day. By nature he was a kindly, generous, impressionable soul, with never a hard word for anyone—unless it were for notorious scoundrels like Regulus. The influence of his uncle and other friends had made a deep impression on him. It was an age when the finer spirits were reaching out towards a higher conception of life. A generation later the philosopher-emperor Marcus Aurelius could write : ' The best way you can avenge yourself is not to do likewise.' ' Love the men among whom your lot is cast—but wholeheartedly.' ' Let any say or do what he will, I must for my part be good.' Men were beginning to put into practice the Stoic doctrine that all men were equal. The treatment of slaves, in particular, was improving ; and Pliny, as we have seen, could show a tactful consideration for his staff by retiring to his study rather than risk embarrassing their merry-making. The following letter reveals his genuine affection for a freed-man secretary suffering from consumption, whom he is sending to recuperate at a friend's sea-side estate on the Italian Riviera.

XXIX Video quam molliter tuos habeas [1] ; quo simplicius tibi confitebor qua indulgentia meos tractem.[2] Est mihi semper in animo hoc nostrum ' pater familiae '.[3] Quod si essem natura asperior et durior, frangeret [4] me tamen infirmitas liberti mei Zosimi. Homo probus, officiosus, litteratus ; et ars quidem ejus comoedus,[5] in qua plurimum facit. Nam pronuntiat acriter, sapienter, apte, decenter etiam ; utitur et cithara perite. Idem tam commode orationes et historias et carmina legit, ut hoc solum didicisse

[1] ' how kindly you treat your servants '.   [2] ' handle '.
[3] ' our national phrase " father of a household " '.
[4] ' melt my heart '.
[5] ' his art is (to be) an entertainer '.

videatur. Haec tibi sedulo exposui, quo magis scires quam multa unus mihi ministeria praestaret. Ille ante aliquot annos, dum intente instanterque pronuntiat, sanguinem rejecit atque ob hoc in Aegyptum missus a me post longam peregrinationem confirmatus rediit nuper ; deinde, dum per continuos dies nimis imperat voci,[6] veteris infirmitatis tussicula admonitus [7] rursus sanguinem reddidit. Qua ex causa destinavi eum mittere in praedia tua, quae Foro Juli possides. Audivi enim te saepe referentem esse ibi et aëra salubrem et lac ejus modi curationibus accommodatissimum.[8] [V 19]

¶ The noblest element in the Romans' character was the high standard of their home-life. Even in the earliest days of the Republic women had been held in special esteem. Wives, so far from being downtrodden household drudges, were the companions and confidantes of their husbands. Some had actually exercised a wholesome influence on public life. It is true that divorces were lightly undertaken, and second or even third marriages were common enough. Pliny himself was twice remarried. His second wife died when he was thirty-six ; Calpurnia, his third wife, is the only one of whom we know much. His correspondence shows that a most sincere devotion existed between them. She went out with him to Bithynia, and in one of his letters to Trajan he apologises for having used the imperial system of post-chaises when she wished to hurry home to Italy on her grandfather's death. Her health was not strong, and when she was forced to go to Campania for a cure, he writes to her with touching anxiety.

XXX C. PLINIUS CALPURNIAE SUAE S.

Scribis te absentia mea non mediocriter adfici unumque habere solacium, quod pro me libellos [1] meos teneas ; saepe

[6] ' makes too great a demand on his voice '.
[7] ' warned of (the return of) his old complaint by a slight cough '.
[8] ' most suitable to cures of this kind '.
XXX [1] ' letters '.

E

etiam in vestigio meo colloces.[2] Gratum est quod nos re-
quiris, quod his fomentis adquiescis.[3] Invicem ego epistulas
tuas lectito atque identidem in manus, quasi novas,[4] sumo ;
sed eo magis ad desiderium tui accendor. Nam, cujus
litterae tantum habent suavitatis, hujus sermonibus quantum
dulcedinis inest ! Tu tamen frequentissime scribe, licet
hoc ita me delectet, ut torqueat.[5] Vale. [VI 7]

℃. Pliny had no children ; it was one of the great disappointments of his life—and this was all the more unfortunate,
since he would have made an excellent father. Here is a
letter which he wrote on hearing of the death of a friend's
daughter. It is touching evidence of his understanding and
appreciation of children.

XXXI Tristissimus haec tibi scribo, Fundani nostri filia
minore defuncta, qua puella nihil umquam festivius,[1]
amabilius, nec longiore vita dignius vidi. Nondum annos
XIII impleverat ; et jam illi anilis prudentia,[2] matronalis
gravitas erat, et tamen suavitas puellaris cum virginali
verecundia. Ut [3] illa patris cervicibus inhaerebat ! Ut nos
amicos paternos et amanter et modeste complectebatur !
Ut nutrices et paedagogos [4] et praeceptores diligebat !
Quam studiose, quam intellegenter lectitabat ! Ut parce
custoditeque ludebat [5] ! Qua patientia, qua etiam constantia novissimam valetudinem [6] tulit ! Duravit illi usque
ad extremum vigor animi, nec aut spatio valetudinis aut
metu mortis infractus est.

[2] ' you set them in my place beside you '.
[3] ' you find relief in these comforts '.
[4] ' as though they were fresh letters '.
[5] ' although this gives me pain as well as pleasure ', lit. ' delights
me in such a way as also to torture me '.
XXXI [1] ' more charming '.   [2] ' an old woman's sense '.
[3] ' how . . . ! '   [4] ' tutors '.
[5] ' how sparingly and with what propriety she took her fun '.
[6] ' last illness '.

O triste acerbumque funus! Non possum exprimere
verbis quantum animo vulnus acceperim, cum audivi
Fundanum ipsum praecipientem, quod in vestes, mar-
garita, gemmas fuerat erogaturus,[7] hoc in tus et unguenta et
odores [a] impenderetur. [V 16]

[a] Incense, unguents and scents were in preparation for the burning of the corpse, which was the custom of the ancient Greeks and
Romans alike. The ashes were afterwards collected and placed
in a tomb or monument erected outside the city, often along one
of the roads.

⁋ Sincerity of character is best tested in a crisis and, if we
really wish to know of what stuff these Romans were made,
it is worth while studying the behaviour of both Pliny and
his uncle during the great catastrophe which cost the latter
his life. All know the story of the sentinel of Pompeii who
was caught upright and unflinching at his post, when the
ashes of Mt Vesuvius overwhelmed and encased him in a
living tomb. There is probably no truth in the tale, but
Pliny's letter at any rate is plain historic fact, and we may
well admire the cool courage with which this eighteen-year-
old boy faced imminent destruction. It was many years
later that his friend Tacitus, wishing to include some account
of the eruption in his *History*, asked Pliny to put down his
memories on paper. The following extracts are drawn from
Pliny's reply.

XXXII *A*. Hora fere septima mater mea indicat ei apparere
nubem inusitata et magnitudine et specie. Poscit soleas,
ascendit locum ex quo maxime miraculum illud conspici
poterat. Nubes ex monte (Vesuvium fuisse postea cognitum
est), oriebatur, cujus formam non alia magis arbor quam
pinus expresserit.[1] Nam longissimo velut trunco elata in
altum, quibusdam ramis diffundebatur. Magnum propi-

[7] ' what he had intended to devote to clothes, pearls, precious
stones '. sc. *ut* after *praecipientem*, ' giving orders that '.

XXXII *A*. [1] ' the shape of which no tree reproduced so well as
a pine-tree '.

usque noscendum eruditissimo viro visum.²   Jubet liburni-
cam aptari ; mihi, si venire una vellem, facit copiam :
respondi studere me malle, et forte ipse quod scriberem

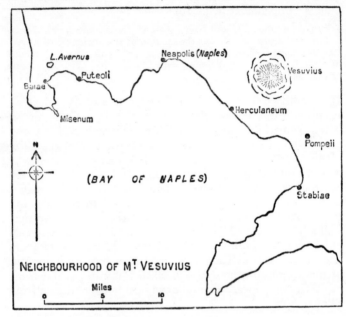

NEIGHBOURHOOD OF M.T VESUVIUS

dederat.   Egrediebatur domo : accipit codicillos ³ Rectinae
imminenti periculo exterritae (nam villa ejus subjacebat nec
ulla nisi navibus fuga) : ut se tanto discrimini eriperet,
orabat.   Vertit ille consilium.   Deducit quadriremes,
ascendit ipse, non Rectinae modo, sed multis laturus auxilium.   Recta gubernacula in periculum tenet, adeo solutus
metu, ut omnes illius mali motus, omnes figuras dictaret
enotaretque.   Jam navibus cinis incidebat, jam pumices

---

¹ ' It seemed to my scholarly uncle an important (phenomenon)
and one which should be inspected at closer quarters.'

² ' as he was leaving, he received a note '.

etiam nigrique et ambusti lapides. Cunctatus paulum, mox
gubernatori ' Fortes ', inquit, ' fortuna juvat : Pomponianum
pete.' Stabiis erat [4]; ibi sarcinas contulerat in naves certus
fugae, si contrarius ventus resedisset. Quo avunculus meus
secundissimo invectus [5] complectitur trepidantem, consol-
atur, hortatur, utque timorem ejus sua securitate leniret,
deferri in balineum jubet : lotus accubat, cenat aut hilaris
aut similis hilari. Tum se quieti dedit et quievit verissimo
quidem somno. Nam meatus animae, qui illi propter ampli-
tudinem corporis gravior et sonantior erat, ab iis, qui limini
obversabantur, audiebatur. Sed area ita jam cinere mixtisque
pumicibus oppleta surrexerat, ut, si longior in cubiculo
mora, exitus negaretur.[6] Excitatus procedit seque Pom-
poniano ceterisque reddit. In commune consultant. Placuit
egredi in litus et ex proximo aspicere ecquid jam mare
admitteret [7]; quod adhuc vastum et adversum [8] permane-
bat. Ibi super abjectum linteum recubans semel atque
iterum frigidam poposcit hausitque. Deinde flammae
odorque sulpuris alios in fugam vertunt, excitant illum.
Innitens servulis duobus adsurrexit et statim concidit,
crassiore caligine spiritu obstructo clausoque stomacho, qui
illi natura invalidus et angustus erat. Ubi dies redditus,
corpus inventum integrum, inlaesum ; habitus corporis
quiescenti quam defuncto similius. [VI 16]

B. Profecto avunculo ipse reliquum tempus studiis (ideo
enim remanseram) impendi : mox balineum, cena, somnus
inquietus et brevis. Praecesserat per multos dies tremor
terrae minus formidolosus, quia Campaniae solitus. Illa
vero nocte ita invaluit ut non moveri omnia sed verti creder-
entur. Inrumpit cubiculum meum mater : surgebam

[4] ' Pomponianus was at Stabiae '.
[5] ' carried by the same wind blowing well behind him '.
[6] ' the courtyard's level was rising so that exit would be impossible '.
[7] ' what the sea would allow of '.
[8] ' rough and running inshore '.

invicem, si quiesceret, excitaturus.[1] Residimus in area
domus. Posco librum Titi Livi et quasi per otium lego
atque etiam, ut coeperam, excerpo. Ecce [2] amicus avunculi
qui nuper ex Hispania venerat, ut me et matrem sedentes,
me vero etiam legentem videt, illius patientiam, securitatem
meam corripit. Nihilo segnius ego intentus in librum.
Jam hora diei prima : jam quassatis tectis, magnus et certus
ruinae metus.[3] Tum demum excedere oppido visum.
Sequitur vulgus attonitum, ingentique agmine abeuntes
premit et impellit.

Egressi tecta [4] consistimus. Multa ibi miranda, multas
formidines patimur. Nam vehicula, quae produci jussera-
mus, quamquam in planissimo campo in contrarias partes
agebantur, ac ne lapidibus quidem fulta in eodem vestigio
quiescebant. Praeterea mare in se resorberi et tremore
terrae repelli videbamus : litus multa animalia maris siccis
harenis detinebat.[5] Ab altero latere nubes atra et horrenda
in longas flammarum figuras dehiscebat [6] ; fulguribus illae
et similes et majores erant. Tum vero ille ex Hispania amicus acrius et instantius, ' si frater ', inquit, ' tuus, tuus avunculus [7] vivit, vult esse vos salvos ; si periit, superstites voluit.
Proinde quid cessatis [8] evadere? ' Non moratus ultra
proripit se effusoque cursu periculo aufertur.[9] Nec multo
post illa nubes descendere in terras, operire maria. Jam
cinis, adhuc tamen rarus ; respicio ; densa caligo tergis
imminebat ; et nox, non qualis inlunis aut nubila, sed qualis
in locis clausis lumine exstincto. Audires [10] ululatus femin-
arum, infantium quiritatus, clamores virorum ; alii parentes,

---

[1] ' I was meaning on my part to wake *her*, if asleep '.
[2] ' Lo and behold ! in comes . . .'
[3] ' a serious and obvious risk of the house falling down '.
[4] ' when we got beyond the houses '.   [5] ' retained '.
[6] ' was rent (lit. yawned) in long fiery streamers '.
[7] i.e. the mother's brother and Pliny's uncle.
[8] ' why hesitate ?'
[9] ' without further delay he rushed out and made his way to safety
at top speed '.
[10] ' one might have heard '.

alii liberos, alii conjuges vocibus requirebant : hi suum
casum, illi suorum miserabantur ; erant qui metu mortis
mortem precarentur ; multi ad deos manus tollere, plures
nusquam jam deos ullos aeternamque et novissimam noctem
mundo interpretabantur.[11]   Tandem illa caligo tenuata
quasi in fumum nebulamve discessit : mox dies verus, sol
etiam effulsit.   Regressi Misenum, curatis corporibus, sus-
pensam noctem spe ac metu exegimus.[12] [VI 20]

¶. It would be absurd to pretend that Pliny was a great man.
In the whole of his correspondence there is not, perhaps, a
single original idea.   Like the majority of men at all epochs
he took his cue from those around him.   He was conventional
even for a Roman, and sometimes conventional to an almost
incredible degree.   Once, when informed that his poems had
been much criticised for their coarseness, he wrote in self-
defence to a friend.   In the best poets, he said, he had found a
good deal of coarseness ; and so had concluded that, if he
wanted to write poetry, it was the ' done thing ' to be coarse.
Whether it was his own inclination or no, was nothing to the
point !

The virtues and the limitations of Pliny's character were
perhaps most vividly revealed by an experience which befell
him during his mission in Bithynia—for he there encountered
a branch of the early Christian Church.   Half a century or
more had now elapsed since St Paul sowed the seed of Chris-
tianity in Asia Minor.   It had taken strong root in Bithynia.
Indeed the number of converts was so large that the pagan
temples were emptied of their worshippers.   The altars of
the old gods no longer reeked with the blood of sacrificial
victims, and farmers who had counted on selling the fodder
for fattening them could no longer find a buyer.

In itself the formation of a new religious sect was no crime ;
the Romans were no bigots, and, when many gods were
worshipped, there was always room, they felt, for one more.

[11] ' explained it as the world's end in final and everlasting night '.
[12] ' spent a night poised between hope and fear '.

Secret societies (*hetaeriae*), on the other hand, they always regarded as politically dangerous ; and Trajan himself had issued orders that these should be suppressed. The attitude of Christians towards the worship of the Emperor was a further count against them. Their beliefs would not permit them to share in such idolatry, and it was easy to interpret their abstention as high treason. Public opinion, too, was on the whole against them. Ugly stories were put round about their secret rites ; one (clearly a misunderstanding of the Holy Communion) declared that they feasted upon human flesh.

In Bithynia, the arrival of the new commissioner appears to have been the signal for a fresh anti-Christian agitation. Pliny began to receive complaints. Many individuals were denounced and brought before him for trial. A long list of suspects was forwarded to him anonymously. Under such circumstances Pliny behaved precisely as we should expect him to behave. He took immense pains to deal correctly with this difficult matter. He examined the accused with scrupulous care, and enquired very exactly into the details of their ritual. He was told how on a certain fixed day (very obviously Sunday) they met before dawn and sang a hymn after the Jewish manner, antiphonally—that is, two groups singing lines or verses alternately ; how they bound themselves by an oath not to steal, not to commit adultery, not to break faith with a neighbour (in other words they repeated the Ten Commandments) ; how finally in the evening they met again for a meal, a ' harmless ' meal of ' ordinary ' food (that is, not human flesh). This was clearly the Love Feast or Agapē, which at this date was no longer associated, as it had been in St Paul's time, with the Communion proper.

To make doubly sure that nothing was being concealed, Pliny further examined under torture two female Christians who held the position of ' deaconesses ' in the Church. His method of finally deciding the issue was simple. He ordered the prisoners to repeat at his dictation a prayer to the pagan gods. He then made them offer incense and wine before the image of the Emperor and simultaneously revile the name of Christ. If they refused, they were led off to execution, or, if Roman citizens, they were reserved for trial before the Emperor's judgment-seat. There remained, however, one or two problems. Were those who had been Christians but had abandoned the faith to be allowed the benefit of the doubt? Were Christians, as such, to be punished, even if guiltless of any illegal practice? Pliny himself had no experience of investigations into such matters. He therefore wrote to ask Trajan's advice.

One problem never seems to have crossed his mind. He never asked himself what these Christians really stood for. Their faith was to him simply ' gross superstition ' (he uses the same word of a man who, in a curious access of religious zeal, poured some oil over the dolphin at Hippo). Their courage was nothing better than ' obstinacy '. That their beliefs were a challenge to his own muddle-headed blend of pagan philosophies, never occurred at all to his conventional Roman mind. His letter remains—one of the most illuminating documents perhaps of all antiquity. It shall here be given in full, with the Emperor's reply.

XXXIII *A.* Sollemne est mihi, domine, omnia de quibus dubito ad te referre. Quis enim potest melius vel cunctationem meam regere vel ignorantiam instruere?[1] Cognitionibus de Christianis interfui numquam : ideo nescio quid et quatenus aut puniri soleat aut quaeri.[2] Nec mediocriter haesitavi, sitne aliquod discrimen aetatum, an quamlibet teneri[3] nihil a robustioribus differant ; detur paenitentiae venia, an ei, qui omnino Christianus fuit, desisse non prosit,[4] nomen ipsum, si flagitiis careat, an flagitia cohaerentia nomini puniantur.

[1] ' guide my perplexity or instruct my ignorance '.
[2] ' what method or degree of punishment or enquiry are usual '.
[3] ' culprits however tender '.
[4] ' it should not benefit them to have discontinued it '.

Interim in iis, qui ad me tamquam Christiani deferebantur, hunc sum secutus modum. Interrogavi ipsos an essent Christiani : confitentes iterum ac tertio interrogavi supplicium minatus : perseverantes duci [5] jussi. Neque enim dubitabam, qualecumque esset quod faterentur, pertinaciam certe et inflexibilem obstinationem debere puniri. Fuerunt alii similis amentiae, quos, quia cives Romani erant, adnotavi in urbem remittendos.

Mox ipso tractatu, ut fieri solet, diffundente se crimine plures species inciderunt. [6] Propositus est libellus sine auctore multorum nomina continens. Qui negabant esse se Christianos aut fuisse, cum praeeunte me deos appellarent et imagini tuae, quam propter hoc jusseram cum simulacris numinum adferri, ture ac vino supplicarent, praeterea male dicerent Christo, quorum nihil posse cogi dicuntur qui sunt re vera Christiani, dimittendos esse putavi. Alii ab indice nominati esse se Christianos dixerunt et mox negaverunt ; fuisse quidem, sed desisse, quidam ante triennium, quidam ante plures annos, non nemo etiam ante viginti. Hi quoque omnes et imaginem tuam deorumque simulacra venerati sunt et Christo male dixerunt. Adfirmabant autem hanc fuisse summam vel culpae suae vel erroris, quod essent soliti stato die ante lucem convenire carmenque Christo quasi deo dicere secum invicem [7] seque sacramento non in scelus aliquod obstringere, sed ne furta, ne latrocinia, ne adulteria committerent, ne fidem fallerent, ne depositum appellati abnegarent [8] : quibus peractis morem sibi discedendi fuisse rursusque coeundi ad capiendum cibum, promiscuum tamen et innoxium ; quod ipsum facere desisse post edictum meum, quo secundum mandata tua hetaerias esse vetueram. Quo magis necessarium credidi ex duabus ancillis, quae

[5] ' led to execution '.

[6] ' presently, as is always the way, the mere handling of the matter led to an increase in the number of charges and new types came to light '.

[7] ' singing verse and verse about '.

[8] ' repudiate a liability, when called upon '.

ministrae dicebantur, quid esset veri et per tormenta quaerere. Nihil aliud inveni quam superstitionem pravam, immodicam.

Ideo dilata cognitione ad consulendum te decucurri. Visa est enim mihi res digna consultatione, maxime propter periclitantium numerum. Multi enim omnis aetatis, omnis ordinis, utriusque sexus etiam, vocantur in periculum et vocabuntur. Neque civitates tantum sed vicos etiam atque agros superstitionis istius contagio pervagata est ; quae videtur sisti et corrigi posse. Certe satis constat prope jam desolata templa coepisse celebrari et sacra sollemnia diu intermissa repeti pastumque venire victimarum, cujus adhuc rarissimus emptor inveniebatur. Ex quo facile est opinari, quae turba hominum emendari possit, si sit paenitentiae locus. [X 96]

B.   TRAJANUS PLINIO

Actum quem debuisti, mi Secunde, in excutiendis causis eorum, qui Christiani ad te delati fuerant, secutus es. Neque enim in universum aliquid, quod quasi certam formam habeat, constitui potest. Conquirendi non sunt : si deferantur et arguantur, puniendi sunt, ita tamen ut qui negaverit se Christianum esse idque re ipsa manifestum fecerit, id est supplicando dis nostris, quamvis suspectus in praeteritum, veniam ex paenitentia impetret. Sine auctore vero propositi libelli in nullo crimine locum habere debent. Nam et pessimi exempli nec nostri saeculi est. [X 97]

MARTIAL : THE EPICUREAN IDEAL

(See page 61)

These, gentle Martial, hold in brief
The secret of the happy life :
Wealth by bequest—not labour—got :
A settled home, a pleasant plot :

Never at law, seldom in town,
Nor need to wear the civic gown :
Calm spirit, constitution good :
The vigour of pure Roman blood :
Wise candour : kindred souls to share
The friendly board and simple fare :
Nights blithe, not fuddled : slumber sound
To bring the morning quickly round :
Content with what you are, my friend,
You'll not desire, nor dread, your end.

SENECA: THE STOIC KING

(See page 61)

Wealth cannot a monarch make,
   Nor diadem on brow,
Purple robe upon the back,
   Nor gilded portico.
King is he whom naught dismays,
   No lust enticeth him,
Scorning ambition's giddy ways
   And the mad mob's whim.
Stroke of lightning falling steep
   Shall not him appal,
Tumult of the vasty deep
   Or the raging squall.
Shock of lance he can despise
   And the battle's roll ;
Every blessing he enjoys,
   Master of his soul.
Fronting fate with courage stout
   Unafraid to die,
Hopes and terrors all forgot,
   Very King is he.
Every man, whate'er his lot,
   Such a King may be.

QUESTIONS

I Write a similar description of any place you are fond of.

II If the Elder Pliny had lived to-day would he have done cross-word puzzles on a journey?

III How would a modern master behave towards his servants at Christmas time?

IV Compare Pliny's day with the day of a twentieth-century Englishman. Would you prefer to read to yourself or be read to?

V Write a letter reproducing Pliny's ideas in your own language.

VI Is there any part of the Commonwealth where a similar atrocity might occur?

VII Which of the two theories advanced in the first sentence is supported by the ghost-story?

VIII Would the town-council of a modern sea-side resort adopt the course described in the last sentence? If not, what would they do?

IX What official of the Roman Empire, mentioned in the New Testament, was amenable to bribery?

X What objection is there to an advocate accepting a fee?

XI In what details of his speech is Pliny's flattery excessive?

XII Would you have expected Pliny to be nervous?

XIII Why did provincials appeal to the Emperor?

XIV What complaints had Pliny made about his ' little body '?

XV Was Trajan more likely to be right or Pliny who was on the spot?

XVI What were the chief attractions of a dinner party at Pliny's?

XVII Did Iavolenus mean to be funny?

XVIII Should the recitation of a poem be accompanied by gesticulation?

PIECE

XIX   Does this letter indicate that Pliny was a selfish man?

XX   In which of these three stories did Regulus adopt the best tactics?

XXI   Does Pliny's criticism apply to modern sport-enthusiasts?

XXII   Draw a picture (or plan) of the view from Pliny's Tuscan house.

XXIII   Why did Pliny go hunting?

XXIV   What equivalent act of munificence might be expected of an English squire? Would his motives be the same as Pliny's?

XXV   Would Pliny have preferred a day-school to a boarding-school? If so, why?

XXVI   Make your own list of the essentials of a happy life.

XXVII   In what points did the Stoic ideal coincide with the Epicurean?

XXVIII   Was Arria really true to the Stoic ideal?

XXIX   What does the first sentence of this letter imply about most Romans' attitude to slaves and freedmen?

XXX   What would you infer from Pliny's words about his wife's letters?

XXXI   Should a young girl possess all the qualities which Pliny attributes to Fundanus' daughter?

XXXII   *A.* Could Pliny's uncle have escaped death?
     B. Describe in your own words an eruption of Vesuvius.

XXXIII   *A.* How would you have dealt with an anonymous accusation?
     B. Did Trajan on the whole approve of Pliny's policy?

VOCABULARY

(Note: Long vowels are marked except (1) where consonants make the syllable necessarily long, and (2) final syllables which follow a recognised rule.)

A

ā, ab, *prep. with abl.*, by, from.

ab-eo, -īre, -ii or **-īvi, -itum,** 4, go away.

ab-icio, -icere, -jēci, -jectum, 3, throw away.

abnego, 1, refuse to acknowledge, deny.

absen-s, -tis, *adj.*, absent.

absentia, 1 *f.*, absence.

absol-vo, -vere, -vi, -ūtum, 3, set free, pay off.

abstinentia, 1 *f.*, abstinence, self-restraint.

ab-sum, -esse, -fui, to be absent.

absū-mo, -mere, -mpsi, -mptum, 3, take away, consume.

abundo, 1, abound.

ac, *conj.*, and.

accen-do, -dere, -di, -sum, 3, kindle.

ac-cipio, -cipere, -cēpi, -ceptum, 3, receive.

accommodātus, *adj.* fitting, beneficial.

accubo, 1, lie down.

accursus, 4 *m.*, a running to.

accūsāt-or, -ōris, 3 *m.*, accuser, prosecutor.

accūso, 1, accuse.

āc-er, -ris, -re, *adj.*, keen.

acerbus, *adj.*, bitter, untimely.

ācriter, *adv.*, keenly.

ācroām-a, -atis, 3 *n.*, something pleasant to hear.

actum, 2 *n.*, deed.

actus, 4 *m.*, course of action.

ad, *prep. with acc.*, to, towards, at.

add-o, -ere, -idi, -itum, 3, add, join, attach.

addū-co, -cere, -xi, -ctum, 3, lead to, bring, induce.

adeo, *adv.*, so, so much, moreover.

ad-eo, -īre, -ii or **-īvi, -itum,** 4, go to, approach.

adf-icio, -icere, -ēci, -ectum, 3, affect, influence.

adfirmo, 1, assert, declare.

adhibeo, 2, hold to, apply, summon.

adhūc, *adv.*, still, yet.

ad-icio, -icere, -jēci, -jectum, 3, add, put against or near.

adjac-eo, -ēre, -ui, 2, lie near, adjoin.

adlocūti-o, -ōnis, 3 *f.*, manner of address.

admi-tto, -ttere, -si, -ssum, 3, admit, receive.

admoneo, 2, remind, suggest, advise, warn.

adnato, 1, swim towards.

adnoto, 1, annotate, comment upon.

adn-uo, -uere, -ui, -ūtum, 3, nod assent, acquiesce.

adopti-o, -ōnis, 3 *f.*, adoption.

adpet-o, -ere, -īvi or **-ii, -ītum,** 3, strive after ; **adpeten-s, -tis,** *adj.*, desirous.

adqui-esco, -escere, -ēvi, -ētum, 3, come to rest, find comfort in.

adsen-tio, -tīre, -si, -sum, 4, assent, approve.

adsiduus, *adj.*, diligent, unceasing, persistent.

ad-sum, -esse, -fui, be present, assist (*with dat.*).

adsur-go, -gere, -rexi, -rectum, 3, rise up.

adulterium, 2 *n.*, adultery.

advento, 1, approach.

adventus, 4 *m.*, approach, arrival.

adversus, *adj.*, contrary to, opposite.

adversus, *prep. with acc.*, against.

advesper-ascit, -āvit, *impers.* 1, evening is coming on.

advocāti-o, -ōnis, 3 *f.*, legal advice, counsel.

advocātus, 2 *m.*, helper, advocate.

aeg-er, -ra, -rum, *adj.*, sick ; **aegrē,** *adv.*, painfully, scarcely.

āēr (*acc.* **āera**), **āeris,** 3 *m.*, air, atmosphere.

aerārium, 2 *n.*, treasury.

ae-s, -ris, 3 *n.*, bronze.

aest-ās, -ātis, 3 *f.*, summer.

aestus, 4 *m.*, tide, heat.

aet-ās, -ātis, 3 *f.*, age.

aeternus, *adj.*, eternal, perennial.

affero, afferre, attuli, allātum, 3, bring to, convey.

ag-er, -ri, 2 *m.*, field, estate.

agitāti-o, -ōnis, 3 *f.*, violent movement, exercise.

agitāt-or, -ōris, 3 *m.*, charioteer.

agito, 1, put in motion, employ.

agm-en, -inis, 3 *n.*, multitude, throng.

ag-nosco, -noscere, -nōvi, -nitum, 3, recognize.

ag-o, -ere, ēgi, actum, 3, do, achieve, plead, act a part ; **quid agit ...?** how fares ...?

agrest-is, -e, *adj.*, rustic ; *as subst.*, peasant.

āla, 1 *f.*, wing, squadron.

alac-er, -ris, -re, *adj.*, lively, eager.

alb-eo, -ēre, —, —, 2, be white.

alibi, *adv.*, elsewhere ; **alibi ... alibi,** here ... there.

alica, 1 *f.*, spelt, porridge.

aliēnus, *adj.*, belonging to another, foreign.

aliōqui, *adv.*, otherwise.

aliquando, *adv.*, at some time or other, once.

aliquanto, *adv.*, somewhat.

aliquantum, 2 *n.*, some amount.

ali-quis, -qua, -quid, *pron.*, someone, anyone.

aliquot, *adj. indecl.*, some, a few.

ali-us, -a, -ud, *adj.*, another, other ; **alii ... alii,** some ... others.

alligo, 1, bind to.

al-o, -ere, -ui, -itum or **-tum,** 3, nourish, support.

alter, -a, -um, *adj.*, the other.

alternus, *adj.*, alternate, mutual.

altus, *adj.*, high, deep ; **altum,** 2 *n.*, the deep, *used for* the sea

alveus, 2 *m.*, hollow, river-bed.

amābil-is, -e, *adj.,* attractive, pleasing.

amanter, *adv.,* lovingly, amiably.

amārus, *adj.,* bitter, sad.

ambiti-o, -ōnis, 3 *f.,* canvassing, ambition, self-seeking.

ambulo, 1, walk.

ambustus, *adj.,* burnt, charred.

āmentia, 1 *f.,* insanity.

amīcus, 2 *m.,* friend.

amn-is, -is, 3 *m.,* river.

amoenit-ās, -ātis, 3 *f.,* charm, delightful view.

amoenus, *adj.,* charming (of scenery).

am-or, -ōris, 3 *m.,* love, favourite.

amphitheātrum, 2 *n.,* amphitheatre.

amplitūd-o, -inis, 3 *f.,* size, stoutness.

amplus, *adj.,* ample, considerable, of high merit.

an, *conj.,* or (*in indirect questions*).

ancilla, 1 *f.,* maidservant.

an-go, -gere, -xi, -ctum, 3, distress, trouble.

angustus, *adj.,* narrow, limited.

anīl-is, -e, *adj.,* of an old woman.

anima, 1 *f.,* breath, soul.

anim-al, -ālis, 3 *n.,* animal.

animus, 2 *m.,* mind.

annus, 2 *m.,* year, season.

ante, *prep. with acc.,* before.

antīquus, *adj.,* ancient, former, old.

aper, apri, 2 *m.,* boar.

aper-io, -īre, -ui, -tum, 4, lay bare, uncover, open.

apparātus, 4 *m.,* preparation, provision, splendour.

appāreo, 2, appear ; **appāret,** *impers.,* it seems, appears.

appello, 1, call upon.

aptē, *adv.,* fitly, suitably, rightly, aptly.

apto, 1, make ready.

apud, *prep. with acc.,* with, at, by, near, at the house of.

aqua, 1 *f.,* water.

arātrum, 2 *n.,* plough.

arbitror, 1 *dep.,* think, deem.

arb-or, -oris, 3 *f.,* tree.

ārea, 1 *f.,* court, space round a house.

arg-uo, -uere, -ui, -ūtum, 3, make clear, prove, censure.

armus, 2 *m.,* shoulder-blade.

ar-s, -tis, 3 *f.,* art, accomplishment, skill.

as, assis, 3 *m.,* as (unit of weight, *or* a coin).

ascen-do, -dere, -di, -sum, 3, mount, climb, ascend.

asper, -a, -um, *adj.,* rough, harsh.

asperit-ās, -ātis, 3 *f.,* roughness, inclemency.

aspernor, 1, *dep.,* disdain.

asp-icio, -icere, -exi, -ectum, 3, look at.

at, *conj.,* but.

āt-er, -ra, -rum, *adj.,* dark, black.

atque, *conj.,* and.

atr-ox, -ōcis, *adj.,* horrible, atrocious.

atten-do, -dere, -di, -tum, 3, stretch or turn towards ; *sc.* **animum,** attend to.

attentus, *adj.,* attentive, careful.

at-tero, -terere, -trīvi, -trītum, 3, wear away, exhaust.

attonitus, *adj.,* bewildered, terrified.

auct-or, -ōris, *c.,* author, promoter.

F

audācia, 1 f., courage, daring, temerity, insolence.

aud-ax, -ācis, adj., spirited, rash, presumptuous.

auden-s, -tis, adj., daring.

audio, 4, hear, listen.

audītus, 4 m., hearing.

au-fero, -ferre, abstuli, ablā-tum, 3, take away, rob of.

au-geo, -gēre, -xi, -ctum, 2, increase.

augurium, 2 n., augury, divination.

augustus, adj., stately, imposing.

aura, 1 f., air, breeze.

aureus, adj., golden, priceless.

aurum, 2 n., gold.

aut, conj., or; aut ... aut, either ... or.

autem, conj., but.

auxilium, 2 n., help, assistance.

avāritia, 1 f., avarice, covetousness.

avunculus, 2 m., uncle.

avus, 2 m., grandfather.

B

balineum, 2 n., bath.

barba, 1 f., beard.

basilica, 1 f., basilica, law-court.

beātus, adj., blessed, happy.

bellum, 2 n., war.

bene, adv., well.

bētāceus, 2 m., beetroot.

bīn-i, -ae, -a, distrib., two by two, two apiece.

bonus, adj., good, kind.

bōs, bovis, 3 c., bull, ox, cow.

brev-is, -e, adj., short, brief.

bulbus, 2 m., onion.

C

cado, cadere, cecidi, cāsum, 3, fall, sink.

caed-o, -ere, cecīdi, caesum, 3, cut, beat, kill.

caeduus, adj., fit for cutting.

caelum, 2 n., heavens, sky.

calco, 1, trample on, tread.

cālīg-o, -inis, 3 f., darkness, mist, cloud.

campus, 2 m., field, plain, level ground.

can-is, -is, 3 c., dog.

cap-ax, -ācis, adj., roomy, capable of holding or keeping.

capillus, 2 m., hair.

capio, capere, cēpi, captum, 3, take, seize.

cap-ut, -itis, 3 n., head.

carc-er, -eris, 3 m., prison.

careo, 2, am without, am free from.

cārit-ās, -ātis, 3 f., dearness, esteem.

carm-en, -inis, 3 n., song, poem.

carp-o, -ere, -si, -tum, 3, pluck, reproach, criticise.

cārus, adj., dear.

castigo, 1, chastise.

castr-a, -orum, 2 n. pl., camp.

cāsus, 4 m., chance, mischance.

catēna, 1 f., chain.

cathedra, 1 f., chair.

causa, 1 f., cause, case (legal).

causā, prep. with abl., for the sake of.

cēd-o, -ere, cessi, cessum, 3, yield.

celeb-er, -ris, -re, adj., public, much frequented.

celebro, 1, keep, celebrate, frequent.

cella, 1 f., room, chamber.

cēna, 1 f., dinner.

cēno, 1, dine, eat.

cens-eo, -ēre, -ui, -um, 2, estimate, deem, move a resolution.

centumvirāl-is, -e, *adj.*, of the *centumviri*.

centumviri, 2 *m. pl.*, civil judges (originally 100).

centuri-o, -ōnis, 3 *m.*, centurion.

cēra, 1 *f.*, wax, wax writing tablet.

certām-en, -inis, 3 *n.*, contest, struggle.

certē, *adv.*, certainly, of a truth.

certus, *adj.*, certain, definite.

cerv-ix, -īcis, 3 *f.*, neck.

cesso, 1, do nothing, loiter, am delayed.

cēteri, *adj.*, the others.

chalyb-s, -is, 3 *m.*, steel.

cibus, 2 *m.*, food, meal.

cin-go, -gere, -xi, -ctum, 3, surround, enclose, shroud.

cin-is, -eris, 3 *m.* (*in sing. sometimes f.*), ashes.

circā, *prep. with acc.*, about, round about, concerning ; *adv.*, all around, near, around.

Circenses (*sc.* ludi), games in the Circus Maximus.

circum-eo, -īre, -īvi or -ii, -itum, 4, go or travel round, canvass.

circum-sisto, -sistere, -stiti or -steti, —, 3, surround.

cithara, 1 *f.*, guitar, lute.

cīv-is, -is, 3 *c.*, citizen.

cīvit-ās, -ātis, 3 *f.*, state, city.

clāmito, 1, call frequently, keep shouting.

clāmo, 1, shout, call.

clām-or, -ōris, 3 *m.*, cry, outcry, noise, applause.

clārit-ās, -ātis, 3 *f.*, brightness, renown.

clārus, *adj.*, bright, renowned, famous.

clau-do, -dere, -si, -sum, 3, shut up, close.

clēmentia, 1 *f.*, mercy, benignity, moderation.

clepsydra, 1 *f.*, water-clock.

clīmactēricus, *adj.*, critical, marking a dangerous period.

cochlea, 1 *f.*, snail.

cōdicill-i, -orum, 2 *m. pl.*, short note, codicil.

co-eo, -īre, -īvi or -ii, -itum, 4, assemble, join.

coep-i, -isse, coeptum, 3, begin.

coerceo, 2, surround, repress, restrain.

cōgitāti-o, -ōnis, 3 *f.*, reflection, thought.

cōgito, 1, reflect upon, consider.

cogniti-o, -ōnis, 3 *f.*, knowledge, inquiry.

cog-nosco, -noscere, -nōvi, -nitum, 3, ascertain, understand.

cōgo, cōgere, coēgi, coactum, 3, drive together, compel.

cohae-reo, -rēre, -si, -sum, 2, stick or cling together.

cohor-s, -tis, 3 *f.*, division, company.

collēgium, 2 *n.*, colleagueship, association in office.

col-ligo, -ligere, -lēgi, -lectum, 3, collect, infer, pick up.

coll-is, -is, 3 *m.*, hill.

colloco, 1, place together.

collum, 2 *n.*, neck.

colōnia, 1 *f.*, settlement.

colōnus, 2 *m.*, settler, tenant.

col-or, -ōris, 3 *m.*, colour.

com-es, -itis, 3 *c.*, associate, companion.

cōmit-ās, -ātis, 3 *f.*, affability, courtesy, kindness.

commendo, 1, commend, recommend.

commīlit-o, -ōnis, 3 *m.*, fellow-soldier.

com-mitto, -mittere, -mīsi, -missum, 3, commit, be guilty of.

commodus, *adj.*, suitable, comfortable, advantageous.

com-moveo, -movēre, -mōvi, -mōtum, 2, move, affect, rouse.

commūn-is, -e, *adj.*, common, general, shared with others.

comparo, 1, compare, get, provide.

comp-ēs, -edis, 3 *f.*, fetter.

compesc-o, -ere, -ui, —, 3, restrain, forbear.

com-plector, -plecti, -plexus sum, 3 *dep.*, embrace, love.

complūr-es, -a, *adj.*, several, some.

com-pōno, -pōnere, -posui, -positum or -postum, 3, compose, put together ; compōno vultum, look grave.

comprehen-do, -dere, -di, -sum, 3, lay hold of, catch.

computo, 1, reckon, calculate.

concē-do, -dere, -ssi, -ssum, 3, yield, resign.

concerp-o, -ere, -si, -tum, 3, pluck, pick up.

concid-o, -ere, -i, —, 3, fall.

concordia, 1 *f.*, union, harmony, concord.

concup-isco, -iscere, -īvi or -ii, -ītum, 3, covet, desire strongly.

concur-ro, -rere, -ri, -sum, 3, come or run together, join battle.

concu-tio, -tere, -ssi, -ssum, 3, shake violently.

condemno, 1, condemn, convict.

cond-o, -ere, -idi, -itum, 3, bring together, compose, hide, found.

condū-co, -cere, -xi, -ctum, 3, lead together, hire, engage.

confero, conferre, contuli, collātum, 3, collect, confer, compare, contribute ; se conferre, betake oneself.

con-ficio, -ficere, -fēci, -fectum, 3, accomplish, exhaust, wear out.

confī-do, -dere, -sus sum, 3 *semi-dep.*, entrust.

confirmo, 1, strengthen, restore to health, confirm.

con-fiteor, -fitēri, -fessus sum, 2 *dep.*, acknowledge, confess.

conflicto, 1, harass, afflict, strike down.

conflu-o, -ere, -xi, —, 3, flow or flock together.

con-junx, -jugis, 3 *c.*, husband, wife.

conquī-ro, -rere, -sīvi, sītum, 3, hunt out.

conscen-do, -dere, -di, -sum, 3, mount, go on board a ship.

con-sentio, -sentīre, -sensi, -sensum, 4, agree, act together.

consilium, 2 *n.*, plan, advice, policy.

con-sisto, -sistere, -stiti, -stitum, 3, stand, stay, stop.

consōlor, 1 *dep.*, comfort.

conspectus, 4 *m.*, view, sight, vision.

con-spicio, -spicere, -spexi, -spectum, 3, perceive, observe.

conspīro, 1, act together.

constantia, 1 *f.*, courage, resolution.

constit-uo, -uere, -ui, -ūtum, 3, establish, appoint, resolve.

const-o, -āre, -iti, -ātum, 1, stand firm, consist of ; constat, *impers.*, it is agreed.

consuētūd-o, -inis, 3 *f.*, custom, habit.

consul, -is, 3 *m.*, consul.

consulār-is, -e, *adj.*, pertaining to a consul.

consul-o, -ere, -ui, -tum, 3, consult.

consultāti-o, -ōnis, 3 *f.*, deliberation, inquiry.

consulto, 1, take counsel.

consultum, 2 *n.*, decree.

consūm-o, -ere, -psi, -ptum, 3, devour, dissipate, consume.

contāgi-o, -ōnis, 3 *f.*, contact, infection.

con-temno, -temnere, -tempsi, -temptum, 3, despise, be indifferent to.

contenti-o, -ōnis, 3 *f.*, controversy, vehement style.

con-tineo, -tinēre, -tinui, -tentum, 2, restrain, comprise.

con-tingo, -tingere, -tigi, -tactum, 3, touch, happen.

continuus, *adj.*, continuous, in unbroken line.

contrā, *prep. with acc.*, against, opposite ; *adv.*, opposite, on the other hand.

con-traho, -trahere, -traxi, -tractum, 3, draw together, contrast, shorten.

contrārius, *adj.*, opposite, contrary.

con-tundo, -tundere, -tudi, -tūsum, 3, crush, bludgeon.

con-venio, -venīre, -vēni, —, 4, be suitable.

con-verto, -vertere, -verti, -versum, 3, turn, turn round.

convictus, 4 *m.*, feast, intercourse.

coopto, 1, choose, elect.

cōpia, 1 *f.*, abundance, plenty, ample supply, opportunity ; *in plur.*, supplies.

Corinthius, *adj.*, Corinthian, of Corinthian bronze.

corp-us, -oris, 3 *n.*, body.

corpusculum, 2 *n.*, little body, dear person.

cor-rigo, -rigere, -rexi, -rectum, 3, correct, reform.

cor-ripio, -ripere, -ripui, -reptum, 3, seize, reprove.

cor-rumpo, -rumpere, -rūpi, -ruptum, 3, tempt, corrupt.

cotīdiē, *adv.*, daily.

crassus, *adj.*, dense.

crēb-er, -ra, -rum, *adj.*, frequent, numerous.

crēbr-esco, -escere, -ui, —, 3, become more frequent, grow louder.

crēd-o, -ere, -idi, -itum, 3, believe, trust in.

crēdulus, *adj.*, credulous, easy of belief.

cresco, crescere, crēvi, crētum, 3, grow, rise.

crīm-en, -inis, 3 *n.*, charge, accusation.

cruciātus, 4 *m.*, torture.

crucio, 1, torture.

crūs, crūris, 3 *n.*, leg.

cryptoporticus, 4 *f.*, covered passage or cloister.

cubiculum, 2 *n.*, rest-room, bedroom.

cucurbita, 1 *f.*, gourd, cucumber.

culpa, 1 *f.*, blame.

cum, *prep. with abl.*, with, in the company of, in connection with ; *conj.*, when, whenever, since, although.

cunctāti-o, -ōnis, 3 *f.*, hesitation.

cunctor, 1 *dep.*, delay.

cunctus, *adj.*, all, every.

cup-io, -ere, -īvi, -ītum, 3, desire eagerly.

cūr, *conj.*, why?

cūra, 1 *f.*, care, attention, anxiety.

cūrāti-o, -ōnis, 3 *f.*, cure, treatment.

cūro, 1, care for, take care of.

curr-o, -ere, cucurri, cursum, 3, run.

currus, 4 *m.*, chariot.

cursus, 4 *m.*, course, journey, race.

curvus, *adj.*, winding, stooping, crooked (morally).

custōdio, 4, guard, maintain.

custōdītē, *adv.*, cautiously.

D

damno, 1, condemn.

dē, *prep. with abl.*, from, by reason of, concerning.

dēbeo, 2, owe, be under obligation to, ought.

dē-cēdo, -cēdere, -cessi, -cessum, 3, depart, die.

decem, *numer.*, ten.

decenter, *adv.*, charmingly.

dēcid-o, -ere, -i, —, 3, fall down or away from.

dē-curro, -currere, -cucurri or **-curri, -cursum,** 3, run down, have recourse to.

dēcu-tio, -tere, -ssi, -ssum, 3, cut down, destroy.

dēdicāti-o, -ōnis, 3 *f.*, dedication.

dēdū-co, -cere, -xi, -ctum, 3, lead away, draw from.

dē-fero, -ferre, -tuli, -lātum, 3, carry down, report, accuse.

dē-fīgo, -fīgere, -fixi, -fixum, 3, fix, entirely take up with.

dē-flecto, -flectere, -flexi, -flexum, 3, turn aside.

dēfun-gor, -gi, -ctus sum, 3 *dep.*, perform ; **dēfunctus,** dead.

de-hisco, -hiscere, -hīvi, —, 3, yawn, be apart.

dein, deinde, *adv.*, then, thereafter.

dēlāt-or, -ōris, 3 *m.*, informer, accuser.

dēlecto, 1, please, charm.

dēlēgo, 1, assign.

dēlībero, 1, consider carefully, resolve.

dēlicātus, *adj.*, capricious, delicate.

dēliciae, 1 *f. pl.*, delight, favourite, luxuries.

dēlīrāti-o, -ōnis, 3 *f.*, giddiness, absurd behaviour.

delphīnus, 2 *m.*, dolphin.

dēmum, *adv.*, at last.

dēnique, *adv.*, at last, thereafter, in fine.

densus, *adj.*, thick, dense, crowded.

dēpositum, 2 *n.*, deposit.

dēprecor, 1 *dep.*, deprecate, beg off.

dēprehen-do, -dere, -di, -sum, 3, seize, find, reproach.

descen-do, -dere, -di, -sum, 3, descend.

dēser-o, -ere, -ui, -tum, 3, leave, abandon.

dēsīderium, 2 *n.*, desire, regret.

dēsīdero, 1, long for, miss.

dēsigno, 1, point out ; **dēsignatus,** *adj.*, designate to an office.

dēsi-no, -nere, -i, -tum, 3, cease.

dēsōlo, 1, desert.

despēro, 1, despair, despair of.

destino, 1, resolve, betroth.

de-stringo, -stringere, -strinxi, -strictum, 3, rub down.

deus, 2 *m.*, god.

dēve-ho, -here, -xi, -ctum, 3, carry off, down, or away.

diaeta, 1 *f.*, way of living, living room.

dī-co, -cere, -xi, -ctum, 3, say.

dicto, 1, assert frequently, dictate.

dies, 5 *m. and f.*, day.

differo, differre, distuli, dīlātum, 3, postpone, differ, disagree.

difficil-is, -e, *adj.*, difficult.

dif-fugio, -fugere, -fūgi, —, 3, fly in different directions.

dif-fundo, -fundere, -fūdi, -fūsum, 3, pour out, spread.

digitus, 2 *m.*, finger.

dignit-ās, -ātis, 3 *f.*, dignity, eminent position.

dignus, *adj. with abl.*, worthy.

dīgre-dior, -di, -ssus sum, 3 *dep.*, depart, leave the room.

dīlā-bor, -bi, -psus sum, 3 *dep.*, glide away, be squandered.

dīlāti-o, -ōnis, 3 *f.*, adjournment, delay.

dīligenter, *adv.*, carefully, diligently.

dīligentia, 1 *f.*, diligence, care.

dī-ligo, -ligere, -lexi, -lectum, 3, value highly, love.

dīluvium, 2 *n.*, flood.

dīmi-tto, -ttere, -si, -ssum, 3, dismiss, despatch.

dīrus, *adj.*, dreadful.

discē-do, -dere, -ssi, -ssum, 3, depart, disperse.

discessi-o, -ōnis, 3 *f.*, division.

disc-o, -ere, didici, —, 3, learn.

discrīm-en, -inis, 3 *n.*, difference, critical moment, crisis.

discursus, 4 *m.*, a running to and fro.

disertus, *adj.*, eloquent.

dis-picio, -picere, -pexi, -pectum, 3, examine.

dis-pōno, -pōnere, -posui, -positum or -postum, 3, arrange, order.

diū, *adv.*, for a long time.

diūtinus, *adj.*, of long duration.

dīversus, *adj.*, opposite, different.

dīv-es, -itis, *adj.*, rich.

dīvīnus, *adj.*, divine, inspired.

do, dare, dedi, datum, 1, give.

doc-eo, -ēre, -ui, -tum, 2, teach, inform.

doleo, 2, feel pain, grieve for.

dominus, 2 *m.*, lord, master.

dom-o, -āre, -ui, -itum, 1, tame, subdue.

domus, 4 *f.*, house, home ; *loc.* domi, at home.

dōnum, 2 *n.*, gift.

dormio, 4, sleep.

dubito, 1, doubt

dubius, *adj.*, doubtful, ambiguous, in suspense.

dū-co, -cere, -xi, -ctum, 3, lead, draw on.

dulcēd-o, -inis, 3 *f.*, sweetness, charm.

dulc-is, -e, *adj.*, sweet, pleasant.

dum, *conj.*, while, as long as, until.

du-o, -ae, -o, *numer.*, two.

dūrē, *adv.*, hardly, rigorously, harshly.

dūro, 1, last, continue.

dūrus, *adj.*, hard, cruel.

E

ē, ex, *prep. with abl.*, out of, from.

ēbrius, *adj.*, drunk.

ecce, *adv.*, behold! lo!

echīnus, 2 *m.*, sea-urchin, hedge-hog.

ec-quis, -quid, *interrog. adj.*, is there anyone who?

ēdictum, 2 *n.*, ordinance, decree.

effero, efferre, extuli, ēlātum, 3, carry out (esp. for burial) ; ēlātus, *adj.*, tall, lofty.

ef-ficio, -ficere, -fēci, -fectum, 3, complete, cause, manage.

effigies, 5 *f.*, likeness, image, phantom.

ef-fingo, -fingere, -finxi, -fictum, 3, fashion, attain.

ef-fodio, -fodere, -fōdi, -fossum, 3, dig up or out.

effulg-eo, -ēre, effulsi, —, 2, shine forth.

ef-fundo, -fundere, -fūdi, -fūsum, 3, pour forth ; effūsus, lavish.

ego, mei, *pron.*, I.

ēgre-dior, -di, -ssus sum, 3 *dep.*, go out or forth.

ēgregius, *adj.*, out of the common herd, distinguished, splendid.

ējusmodi, *indecl. adj.*, such, of that kind.

elegi, 2 *m. pl.*, elegiac verses.

ē-ligo, -ligere, -lēgi, -lectum, 3, choose.

ē-loquor, -loqui, -locūtus sum, 3 *dep.*, speak out, pronounce ; ēloquens, *adj.*, eloquent ; ēloquenter, *adv.*, eloquently.

ēmendo, 1, improve, reform.

emo, emere, ēmi, emptum, 3, buy.

empt-or, -ōris, 3 *m.*, purchaser.

enim, *conj.*, for.

ēnoto, 1, note down.

eo, īre, īvi or ii, itum, 4, go.

epistula, 1 *f.*, letter.

epulum, 2 *n.*, banquet ; *plur. f.*, epulae.

equ-es, -itis, 3, *m.*, horseman, knight, member of class of Equites.

equest-er, -ris, -re, *adj.*, on horseback, equestrian.

equidem, *adv.*, for my part.

equus, 2 *m.*, horse.

ergo, *adv.*, therefore, exactly.

ē-ripio, -ripere, -ripui, -reptum, 3, snatch away, rob.

ērogo, 1, spend.

err-or, -ōris, 3 *m.*, error, mistake.

ērudītus, *adj.*, well-read, learned.

etēsiae, 1 *m. pl.*, Etesian winds.

etiam, *conj.*, also, and, even.

eurīpus, 2 *m.*, narrow channel.

eurus, 2 *m.*, east wind.

ēvā-do, -dere, -si, -sum, 3, go forth, escape, turn out.

ē-venio, -venīre, -vēni, -ventum, 4, come out, happen.

ēvigilo, 1, wake up, awaken.

ēvoco, 1, call forth, summon.

exanim-is, -e, *adj.*, lifeless.

exauctōro, 1, dismiss, discharge.

ex-cēdo, -cēdere, -cessi, -cessum, 3, go beyond or out, exceed, die.

excelsus, *adj.*, lofty, high, sublime.

excerp-o, -ere, -si, -tum, 3, make extracts.

ex-cipio, -cipere, -cēpi, -ceptum, 3, receive, catch, welcome, except.

excito, 1, rouse, quicken, awaken.

excūso, 1, excuse, dispense with, acquit.

ex-cutio, -cutere, -cussi, -cussum, 3, shake out, examine (of accounts).

exemplum, 2 *n.*, example, precedent.

exerceo, 2, practise, harass, till.

ex-haurio, -haurīre, -hausi, -haustum, 4, drain, exhaust.

ex-igo, -igere, -ēgi, -actum, 3, require, demand, spend (time).

exiguus, *adj.*, scanty, limited.

exilium, 2 *n.*, exile.

ex-imo, -imere, -ēmi, -emptum, 3, take out or from.

existimo, 1, consider, think.

exitus, 4 *m.*, issue, result.

expedio, 4, release, free.

experīmentum, 2 *n.*, trial, test, experiment.

ex-perior, -perīri, -pertus sum, 4 *dep.*, test, try, prove.

explic-o, -āre, -āvi or **-ui, -ātum** or **-itum**, 1, explain, set forth.

ex-pōno, -pōnere, -posui, -positum or **-postum**, 3, expound, set before.

ex-primo, -primere, -pressi, -pressum, 3, depict, express.

exsil-io, -īre, -ui, —, 4, jump out of.

exspectāti-o, -ōnis, 3 *f.*, waiting, anticipation.

exspecto, 1, expect, wait for.

ex-stinguo, -stinguere, -stinxi, -stinctum, 3, extinguish, cut off.

exstru-o, -ere, -xi, -ctum, 3, pile up, erect.

ex-tendo, -tendere, -tendi, -tentum or **-tensum**, 3, extend, expand, prolong; **extentus**, *adj.*, extended, stretched wide.

exterreo, 2, alarm.

ex-traho, -trahere, -traxi, -tractum, 3, draw or wrench out.

extrēmus, *adj.*, extreme, final; **ad extrēmum**, to the end.

F

fab-er, -ri, 2 *m.*, workman, craftsman.

fābula, 1 *f.*, story, anecdote.

facies, 5 *f.*, face, appearance, scenery.

facil-is, -e, *adj.*, easy, affable, approachable.

facio, facere, fēci, factum, 3, make, do; **nōtum facio**, make known.

facti-o, -ōnis, 3 *f.*, faction, party, party dispute.

factum, 2 *n.*, deed.

facult-ās, -ātis, 3 *f.*, capacity, wealth.

fallo, fallere, fefelli, falsum, 3, cheat, deceive, escape notice.

falsus, *adj.*, false.

fāma, 1 *f.*, fame, reputation, report.

familia, 1 *f.*, household.

familiār-is, -e, *adj.*, belonging to the household, intimate.

famula, 1 *f.*, handmaid, female slave.

fateor, fatēri, fassus sum, 2 *dep.*, confess.

fātum, 2 *n.*, fate, chance.

fauc-es, -ium, 3 *f. pl.*, throat.

fav-eo, -ēre, fāvi, fautum, 2, favour, support (*with dat.*).

fav-or, -ōris, 3 *m.*, favour, support, partisanship.

febrĭcula, 1 *f.*, slight fever.

fēl-ix, -ĭcis, *adj.*, happy, fortunate.

fēmina, 1 *f.*, woman.

fenestra, 1 *f.*, window.

ferē, *adv.*, almost.

fero, ferre, tuli, lātum, 3, bear, report, extol, achieve.

ferrum, 2 *n.*, iron, sword.

fertilit-ās, -ātis, 3 *f.*, fertility.

ferus, *adj.*, wild, fierce, barbarous.

ferven-s, -tis, *adj.* (*partic. of* **ferveo**), hot.

festīvus, *adj.*, gay, pleasing.

festus, *adj.*, joyful, merry, gay.

fidēl-is, -e, *adj.*, faithful, trusty.

fides, 5 *f.*, faith.

fidūcia, 1 *f.*, confidence.

figūra, 1 *f.*, figure, shape, expression.

fīlia, 1 *f.*, daughter.

fīlius, 2 *m.*, son.

fīn-is, -is, 3 *m.*, boundary, limit ; *plur.*, territories, lands.

fīo, fieri, factus sum, *semi-dep.* (*pass. of* **facio**), be made, become.

firmit-ās, -ātis, 3 *f.*, firmness, strength, vigour.

firmus, *adj.*, strong, resolute.

flāgitium, 2 *n.*, disgrace, misdeed.

flamma, 1 *f.*, flame.

fle-cto, -ctere, -xi, -ctum, 3, bend.

flōridus, *adj.*, in bloom, flowering.

fluito, 1, float.

flūm-en, -inis, 3 *n.*, current, river.

focilo, 1, resuscitate.

focus, 2 *m.*, hearth, home.

fodio, fodere, fōdi, fossum, 3, dig, excavate.

foedus, *adj.*, foul, horrible, disgraceful.

folium, 2 *n.*, leaf.

fōmentum, 2 *n.*, consolation, soothing.

fon-s, -tis, 3 *m.*, fountain, spring.

for-is, -is, 3 *f.*, door, gate ; *generally pl.*

forma, 1 *f.*, form, shape, character.

formīd-o, -inis, 3 *f.*, fear, alarm.

formīdolōsus, *adj.*, terrifying.

formo, 1, shape, compose, train.

forsitan, *adv.*, perhaps.

fortasse, *adv.*, perhaps, possibly, probably.

forte, *adv.*, by chance, as it happens.

fort-is, -e, *adj.*, strong, powerful.

fortūna, 1 *f.*, fortune, chance, wealth.

Forum Jūlii, Roman station of S.E. France, now Fréjus.

fossa, 1 *f.*, ditch, trench.

frag-or, -ōris, 3 *m.*, noise, din.

frango, frangere, frēgi, fractum, 3, break, break in, master.

frāt-er, -ris, 3 *m.*, brother.

frequenter, *adv.*, frequently.

frequento, 1, frequent, visit, attend.

fretum, 2 *n.*, gulf, channel, strait.

frīgidus, *adj.*, cold, insipid, trivial.

frīg-us, -oris, 3 *n.*, cold.

fron-s, -tis, 3 *f.*, front, forehead.

fru-or, -i, -ctus sum, 3 *dep.,* enjoy (*with abl.*).

(frux), frūgis, 3 *f.,* fruit, herbs, advantage.

fuga, 1 *f.,* flight, escape.

fugio, fugere, fūgi, fugitum, 3, flee, avoid, escape.

fulg-ur, -uris, 3 *n.,* lightning.

fulm-en, -inis, 3 *n.,* thunderbolt.

fultus, propped, supported ; *partic. of* **fulc-io, -īre, fulsi, fultum.**

fūmus, 2 *m.,* smoke.

fun-gor, -gi, -ctus sum, 3 *dep.,* perform, discharge (*with abl.*).

fūn-us, -eris, 3 *n.,* obsequies, burial.

furtum, 2 *n.,* theft.

fust-is, -is, 3 *m.,* cudgel, club.

G

gaude-o, -ēre, gāvīsus sum, 2 *semi-dep.,* rejoice, delight in.

gaudium, 2 *n.,* joy, pleasure.

gelidus, *adj.,* cold, freezing.

gemma, 1 *f.,* jewel, bud.

gemmeus, *adj.,* sparkling.

gen-er, -eri, 2 *m.,* son-in-law.

gen-us, -eris, 3 *n.,* kind, class.

gero, gerere, gessi, gestum, 3, wear, wage, do ; **sē gerere,** to behave oneself.

gestāti-o, -ōnis, 3 *f.,* exercise, promenade.

glēba, 1 *f.,* clod, soil.

glōria, 1 *f.,* reputation, fame, boast.

gracilit-ās, -ātis, 3 *f.,* slenderness, grace, simplicity.

gradus, 4 *m.,* step, rank, degree.

graecus, *adj.,* Greek.

grātia, 1 *f.,* grace, charm, gratitude.

grātus, *adj.,* pleasing, welcome.

grav-is, -e, *adj.,* heavy, serious, considerable.

gravit-ās, -ātis, 3 *f.,* gravity, weight.

graviter, *adv.,* heavily, weightily.

gubernāculum, 2 *n.,* helm.

gubernāt-or, -ōris, 3 *m.,* helmsman.

gusto, 1, taste, take a light meal

H

habeo, 2, have, possess.

habitāti-o, -ōnis, 3 *f.,* lodging.

habitus, 4 *m.,* fashion, guise.

haesito, 1, hesitate.

harēna, 1 *f.,* sand.

hau-rio, -rīre, -si, -stum, 4, drain, exhaust, drink.

hēliocamīnus, 2 *m.,* sun-parlour.

herba, 1 *f.,* grass, foliage, herbage.

hērēdit-ās, -ātis, 3 *f.,* inheritance.

hēr-ēs, -ēdis, *c.,* heir or heiress.

hetaeria, 1 *f.,* guild, fraternity, political club.

heus ! *interj.,* what, sir! hullo!

hĭc, haec, hōc, *pron. and adj.,* this.

hīc, *adv.,* here.

hiems, hiemis, 3 *f.,* winter.

hilar-is, -e, *adj.,* blithe, cheerful.

hinc, *adv.,* hence, from this place.

historia, 1 *f.,* narrative, history

hodiē, *adv.,* to-day.

hom-o, -inis, 3 *m.,* man, human being.

honestus, *adj.,* worthy, honourable, noble.

hon-or, -ōris, 3 *m.,* repute, esteem, mark of esteem, high position.

hōra, 1 *f.*, hour, season.

horren-s, -tis, *partic. of* horreo, rough ; horrendus, *gerund-ive*, terrific.

hortor, 1 *dep.*, exhort, encourage.

hūc, *adv.*, hither ; hūc illūc, hither and thither.

hūmānit-ās, -ātis, 3 *f.*, qualities of mankind ; humane, gentle, or courteous conduct.

humerus, 2 *m.*, shoulder.

humil-is, -e, *adj.*, humble, lowly.

I

ibi, *adv.*, in that place, there.

īdem, eadem, idem, *adj.*, the same.

identidem, *adv.*, repeatedly.

ideo, *adv.*, therefore.

ign-is, -is, 3 *m.*, fire.

ignōrantia, 1 *f.*, ignorance.

ill-e, -a, -ud, *pron. and adj.*, that.

illūc, *adv.*, thither.

imāginor, 1 *dep.*, picture to oneself.

imāg-o, -inis, 3 *f.*, likeness, picture, image, bust.

immānit-ās, -ātis, 3 *f.*, monstrous size, monstrous cruelty.

immensus, *adj.*, immense, huge.

immin-eo, -ēre, —, —, 2, hang over, threaten (*with dat.*).

immīt-is, -e, *adj.*, harsh, cruel.

im-mitto, -mittere, -mīsi, -missum, 3, send into, set loose, make to flow.

immo, *adv.*, yes indeed, nay rather.

immōbil-is, -e, *adj.*, motionless, immovable.

immodicus, *adj.*, immoderate, excessive.

immortāl-is, -e, *adj.*, immortal, not to be forgotten, historic.

immōtus, *adj.*, unmoved, calm.

im-pello, -pellere, -puli, -pulsum, 3, drive on, induce, stimulate.

impendium, 2 *n.*, expense, charge, cost.

impen-do, -dere, -di, -sum, 3, weigh, spend.

imperāt-or, -ōris, 3 *m.*, general, emperor.

imperītus, *adj.*, unskilled.

imperium, 2 *n.*, power, rule.

impero, 1, command (*with dat.*); requisition.

impetro, 1, gain by asking.

impetus, 4, attack, violent impulse.

im-pingo, -pingere, -pēgi, -pactum, 3, strike against.

impl-eo, -ēre, -ēvi, -ētum, 2, fill, fill up, complete.

implic-o, -āre, -āvi, -ātum, also -ui, -itum, 1, twine, tangle.

im-pōno, -pōnere, -posui, -positum, 3, put upon, impose upon.

importo, 1, carry in, carry.

impoten-s, -tis, *adj.*, weak, unbridled.

in, *prep. with acc.*, into, against ; *with abl.*, in, among.

inān-is, -e, *adj.*, empty, trivial, unimportant.

incal-esco, -escere, -ui, —, 3, grow hot.

incautus, *adj.*, incautious, care-free.

incendium, 2 *n.*, fire, conflagration.

in-cido, -cidere, -cidi, -cāsum, 3, light upon, fall in with, occur.

in-cipio, -cipere, -cēpi, -ceptum, 3, begin.

incitāmentum, 2 n., spur, stimulus.

incol-o, -ere, -ui, —, 3, inhabit.

incolum-is, -e, adj., safe and sound, in good health.

incrēdibil-is, -e, adj., incredible, wondrous.

in-cumbo, -cumbere, -cubui, -cubitum, 3, lean on, devote oneself to.

inde, adv., then, next.

ind-ex, -icis, c., indicator, index.

indico, 1, point out, indicate.

indū-co, -cere, -xi, -ctum, 3, lead into, induce, bring to.

indulgentia, 1 f., indulgence, forbearance, tenderness.

ind-uo, -uere, -ui, -ūtum, 3, put on.

in-eo, -īre, -īvi or -ii, -itum, 4, enter upon, go into.

inerro, 1, wander in or among, haunt.

inertia, 1 f., laziness, slackness.

infām-is, -e, adj., with a bad name or reputation.

infan-s, -tis, 3 c., infant, child.

in-fero, -ferre, -tuli, illātum, 3, bear or bring into.

infirmit-ās, -ātis, 3 f., bodily weakness, ailment.

inflexibil-is, -e, adj., inflexible.

in-fringo, -fringere, -frēgi, -fractum, 3, break, lessen.

ingenium, 2 n., character, talent, natural ability.

ingen-s, -tis, adj., huge, vast.

ingenuus, adj., free born, (so) worthy of a free man.

ingrātus, adj., thankless, ungrateful.

ingravesc-o, -ere, —, —, 3, grow heavy, become worse.

ingre-dior, -di, -ssus sum, 3 dep., enter, go in, begin.

inhabito, 1, inhabit.

inhae-reo, -rēre, -si, -sum, 2, cling to, cleave to.

inhibeo, 2, keep back, check.

initium, 2 n., beginning.

inlaesus, adj., unhurt, intact.

inlūn-is, -e, adj., moonless.

innato, 1, swim in, float, flow over.

in-nītor, -nīti, -nixus or -nīsus sum, 3 dep., lean upon.

innocen-s, -tis, adj., innocent.

innocentia, 1 f., innocence.

innoxius, adj., harmless, innocent.

inn-uo, -uere, -ui, -ūtum, 3, nod to, sign to.

inopīnātus, adj., unexpected.

in-quam (-quis, -quit, etc.), defect. verb, say.

inquiēto, 1, disturb.

inquiētus, adj., uneasy, disturbed.

in-rumpo, -rumpere, -rūpi, -ruptum, 3, invade, rush into.

insalūbr-is, -e, adj., unhealthy.

in-sero, -serere, -serui, -sertum, 3, insert, place in.

insil-io, -īre, -ui, —, 4, leap upon.

in-sisto, -sistere, -stiti, —, 3, rest or stand upon.

insitus, adj., inborn, fixed, innate.

insolen-s, -tis, adj., contrary to custom, arrogant.

insolitus, adj., unwonted.

inson-o, -āre, -ui, —, 1, rattle.

in-spicio, -spicere, -spexi, -spectum, 3, look into, inspect.

instanter, *adv.*, pressingly, urgently, earnestly.

instit-uo, -uere, -ui, -ūtum, 3, establish, train, determine.

inst-o, -āre, -iti, -ātum, 1, press upon, persist, come upon.

instrūmentum, 2 *n.*, apparatus.

instr-uo, -uere, -uxi, -uctum, 3, instruct, build, furnish.

in-sum, -esse, -fui, to be in or on, belong to.

integ-er, -ra, -rum, *adj.*, untouched, unimpaired.

integrit-ās, -ātis, 3 *f.*, soundness, honesty, integrity.

intell-ego, -egere, -exi, -ectum, 3, ascertain, discern.

intellegenter, *adv.*, intelligently.

inten-do, -dere, -di, -tum or -sum, 3, stretch, aim, employ.

intentē, *adv.*, vigorously.

intentus, *adj.*, intent.

inter, *prep. with acc.*, among, between.

interdī-co, -cere, -xi, -ctum, 3, speak between, prohibit.

interdum, *adv.*, now and again, sometimes.

inter-ficio, -ficere, -fēci, -fectum, 3, kill.

interim, *adv.*, meanwhile.

interior, *adj.*, inner ; interiōra, inner rooms or parts.

interjac-eo, -ēre, —, —, 2, to lie between.

inter-jacio, -jacere, -jēci, -jectum, 3, throw between.

inter-mitto, -mittere, -mīsi, -missum, 3, intermit, place in between.

interpellāti-o, -ōnis, 3 *f.*, interruption.

interpretor, 1 *dep.*, expound, interpret.

interrogo, 1, ask, enquire, examine.

inter-sum, -esse, -fui, be present at, have part in ; interest, it concerns.

inter-venio, -venīre, -vēni, -ventum, 4, come between, occur.

intrā, *prep. with acc.*, within ; *also adv.*

intro, 1, go into, enter.

intum-esco, -escere, -ui, 3, swell up, be puffed up.

inumbro, 1, overshadow.

inūsitātus, *adj.*, unusual.

invā-do, -dere, -si, -sum, 3, attack, rush at.

inval-esco, -escere, -ui, —, 3, increase, prevail.

invalidus, *adj.*, weak, impotent, infirm.

inve-ho, -here, -xi, -ctum, 3, carry into ; *pass.*, sail into.

in-venio, -venīre, -vēni, -ventum, 4, light on, meet with, find.

invicem, *adv.*, in turn.

in-video, -vidēre, -vīdi, -vīsum, 2, envy (*with dat.*)

invidia, 1 *f.*, jealousy, unpopularity, enmity.

invīto, 1, summon, invite, entertain.

invītus, *adj.*, unwilling.

ips-e, -a, -um, *pron. and adj.*, self.

irreligiōsus, *adj.*, impious, sacrilegious.

is, ea, id, *pron. and adj.*, he, she, it, the one mentioned.

ist-e, -a, -ud, *pron. and adj.*, this, that, he, she.

istīc, *adv.*, there, in that place.

ita, *adv.*, thus, in this way ; *of degree*, so, so much.

itaque, *conj.*, and so, therefore, accordingly.
it-er, -ineris, 3 *n.*, journey, road, way.
iterum, *adv.*, again.

J

jac-eo, -ēre, -ui, —, 2, lie, lie down.
jacio, jacere, jēci, jactum, 3, throw.
jaculāti-o, -ōnis, 3 *f.*, javelin throwing.
jam, *adv.*, now, already.
jocus, 2 *m.* (*pl. usually* joca, *n.*), joke.
jubeo, jubēre, jussi, jussum, 2, order.
jūcundus, *adj.*, pleasant.
jūd-ex, -icis, 3 *m.*, judge, juryman.
jūdico, 1, examine, pass judgment, decide.
jun-go, -gere, -xi, -ctum, 3, join, connect, unite.
jūro, 1, swear.
jūs, jūris, 3 *n.*, oath, law, rights.
justitia, 1 *f.*, fairness, justice.
justus, *adj.*, just, fair, reasonable.
juven-is, -e, *adj.*, young.
juvo, juvare, jūvi, jūtum, 1, assist, please.

K

Kalend-ae, -arum, 1 *f. pl.*, first day of the month.

L

lab-or, -ōris, 3 *m.*, work, hardship.
labrum, 2 *n.*, lip.
lac, lactis, 3 *n.*, milk.
lactūca, 1 *f.*, lettuce.
lacus, 4 *m.*, lake.

laetor, 1 *dep.*, rejoice.
laetus, *adj.*, joyous, blooming, fertile.
laguncula, 1 *f.*, small flask.
lancea, 1 *f.*, spear.
lap-is, -idis, 3 *m.*, stone.
latīnus, *adj.*, Latin, of the Latin tongue.
latrōcinium, 2 *n.*, highway robbery.
lātus, *adj.*, wide ; lātē, *adv.*, far and wide.
lat-us, -eris, 3 *n.*, side.
laudo, 1, praise.
laurus, 2 *f.*, laurel.
lau-s, -dis, 3 *f.*, praise, renown.
lautus, *adj.*, luxurious, delicious.
lav-o, -āre, lāvi, lavātum, lautum or lōtum, 1, wash.
lectito, 1 *freq.*, read again and again, habitually.
lect-or, -ōris, 3, *m.*, reader.
lēgātus, 2 *m.*, legate, ambassador, lieutenant, deputy.
lēgo, 1, depute, bequeath ; lēgātum, 2 *n.*, legacy.
leg-o, -ere, lēgi, lectum, 3, collect, choose, read.
lēnio, 4, soothe.
lentus, *adj.*, slow.
lev-is, -e, *adj.*, light ; leviter, *adv.*, lightly.
lex, lēgis, 3 *f.*, law.
libellus, 2 *m.*, little book.
liben-s, -tis, *adj.*, willing, with readiness.
lib-er, -ri, 2 *m.*, book.
līberālit-ās, -ātis, 3 *f.*, generosity.
līber-i, -ōrum, 2 *m. plur.*, children.
lībertus, 2 *m.*, freedman.
lib-et, -uit, 2 *impers.*, it pleases, it is one's wish.

liburnica, 1 *f.*, yacht, galley.
licentia, 1 *f.*, freedom, licence, leave.
lic-et, -uit, 2, it is permitted, lawful (*with dat.*) ; *conj.* (*with subj.*), although.
ligo, 1, tie, bind.
līm-en, -inis, 3 *n.*, threshold.
linteum, 2 *n.*, linen, sail.
līs, lītis, 3 *f.*, quarrel, lawsuit.
litter-ae, -ārum, 1 *f. pl.*, a letter.
litterātus, *adj.*, well-educated.
līt-us, -oris, 3 *n.*, shore.
locupl-es, -ētis, *adj.*, rich.
locus, 2 *m.*, place, position.
longus, *adj.*, long, protracted ; **longē,** *adv.*, far.
loqu-or, -i, locūtus sum, 3 *dep.*, speak.
lūcubro, 1, work or compose by lamplight.
lū-do, -dere, -si, -sum, 3, play, jest, play the fool.
lūm-en, -inis, 3 *n.*, light, eye.
lūsus, 4 *m.*, game, sport.
lux, lūcis, 3 *f.*, light.
lyrist-ēs, -ae, 1 *m.*, lute-player.

M

macies, 5 *f.*, emaciation, leanness.
maculo, 1, stain, defile.
magis, *adv.*, more.
magistrātus, 4 *m.*, magistrate.
magnitūd-o, -inis, 3 *f.*, size, nobility, importance.
magnopere, *adv.*, greatly.
magnus, *adj.*, great, important.
majōr-es, -um, 3 *m. pl.*, ancestors.
mālo, malle, mālui, prefer.
malum, 2 *n.*, evil, temptation.
malus, *adj.*, bad, evil ; **male,** *adv.*, badly, wretchedly.

mandātum, 2 *n.*, charge, order
man-eo, -ēre, -si, -sum, 2, remain, await.
manicae, 1 *f. pl.*, sleeves, gloves.
manifestus, *adj.*, clear.
mansuētūd-o, -inis, 3 *f.*, gentleness, tameness.
manus, 4 *f.*, hand.
mar-e, -is, 3 *n.*, sea.
margarīta, 1 *f.*, pearl.
marītus, 2 *m.*, husband.
māt-er, -ris, 3 *f.*, mother.
mātrōnāl-is, -e, *adj.*, pertaining to a middle-aged woman.
maximē, *adv.*, very greatly, especially.
meātus, 4 *m.*, movement.
med-eor, -ēri, —, 2 *dep.*, heal, cure.
medicus, 2 *m.*, doctor.
mediocriter, *adv.*, ordinarily, tolerably.
Mediōlānum, 2 *n.*, a town of Lombardy, now Milan.
mediterrāneus, *adj.*, inland.
meditor, 1 *dep.*, think over, meditate, consider.
medius, *adj.*, middle, moderate.
melius, *adv.*, better.
memin-i, -isse, *perf. form*, remember (*with gen.*).
men-s, -tis, 3 *f.*, mind, intellect.
mensa, 1 *f.*, table, fare.
merc-ēs, -ēdis, 3 *f.*, reward, price.
merg-o, -ere, mersi, mersum, 3, immerse ; *pass.*, dive.
mess-is, -is, 3 *f.*, harvest.
metallum, 2 *n.*, metal, mine.
met-uo, -uere, -ui, 3, fear.
metus, 4 *m.*, fear.
meus, *adj.*, my.
mīl-es, -itis, 3 *m.*, soldier.
mīlitār-is, -e, *adj.*, military.
mīlito, 1, serve in the field.

mille, *adj. num.*, a thousand ; *plur.*, mīl-ia, -ium, thousands.

Minerva, 1 *f.*, Minerva, goddess of wisdom and learning.

minimum, *adv.*, very little, as little as possible.

ministerium, 2 *n.*, service.

ministra, 1 *f.*, serving-woman, minister.

min-or, -ōris, *adj. comp.*, smaller ; minus, *adv.*, less.

minor, 1 *dep.*, threaten.

mīrāculum, 2 *n.*, wonderful thing, miracle.

mīror, 1 *dep.*, admire, wonder at.

mīrus, *adj.*, strange, wonderful.

misc-eo, -ēre, -ui, mistum or mixtum, 2, mix, mingle.

miser, -a, -um, *adj.*, wretched.

miseror, 1 *dep.*, bewail, pity.

mitto, mittere, mīsi, missum, 3, send.

moderāti-o, -ōnis, 3 *f.*, moderation, restraint.

modestē, *adv.*, moderately.

modicus, *adj.*, moderate, temperate, slight.

modo, *adv.*, only.

modus, 2 *m.*, measure, mode, manner.

moll-is, -e, *adj.*, tender, soft, yielding.

molliter, *adv.*, tenderly, softly.

moneo, 2, advise, warn.

mon-s, -tis, 3 *m.*, mountain, hill.

monstrum, 2 *n.*, portent, apparition, monster.

mora, 1 *f.*, delay.

morbus, 2 *m.*, disease, illness.

mor-ior, -i, mortuus sum, 3 *dep.*, die.

moror, 1 *dep.*, delay, remain.

mor-s, -tis, 3 *f.*, death.

mōs, mōris, 3 *m.*, habit, practice ; mōres, character.

mōtus, 4 *m.*, movement, exercise, impulse.

mov-eo, -ēre, mōvi, mōtum, 2, move, stir.

mox, *adv.*, soon.

mūlier, -is, 3 *f.*, woman.

mulsum, 2 *n.*, mead.

multo, *adv.*, much.

multus, *adj.*, much, many.

mundus, 2 *m.*, universe.

mundus, *adj.*, neat, clean.

mūni-ceps, -cipis, 3 *c.*, inhabitant of free town, fellow citizen.

mūnificus, *adj.*, munificent, generous.

mūnio, 4, fortify, protect, shelter.

murmur, -is, 3 *n.*, murmur.

mūto, 1, change.

mūtus, *adj.*, dumb, speechless.

mūtuus, *adj.*, reciprocal, mutual.

myrtus, 2 *f.*, myrtle.

N

nam, *conj.*, for.

narro, 1, recount, tell.

nasc-or, -i, nātus sum, 3 *dep.*, am born.

nātāl-is, -e, *adj.*, natal ; *as subst. sc.* dies, birthday.

nato, 1, swim.

nātūra, 1 *f.*, nature, disposition.

nāvicula, 1 *f.*, a little boat.

nāvigābil-is, -e, *adj.*, navigable.

nāvigāti-o, -ōnis, 3 *f.*, sailing, navigation.

nāvigium, 2 *n.*, ship.

nāvigo, 1, sail.

nāv-is, -is, 3 *f.*, ship.

nē, *conj.*, lest.

G

-ne, *enclitic interrog. particle.*

nebula, 1 *f.*, mist.

nec, neque, *conj.*, neither, nor.

necessārius, *adj.*, necessary.

neglegentia, 1 *f.*, neglect, heedlessness.

negle-go, -gere, -xi, -ctum, 3, neglect, pay no heed to.

nego, 1, deny.

negōtium, 2 *n.*, business.

nēmo (nullius), 3 *c.*, nobody.

nem-us, -oris, 3 *n.*, wood.

nempe, *conj.*, without doubt.

nept-is, -is, 3 *f.*, granddaughter.

nescio, 4, be ignorant of, not know.

nescio-quis, -quid, *pron.*, someone or other.

neut-er, -ra, -rum, *adj.*, neither the one nor the other.

nēve, *conj.*, and that not.

Nīcomēdia, 1 *f.*, capital of Bithynia.

nig-er, -ra, -rum, *adj.*, black.

nihil, *n. indecl.*, nothing.

nihilō, *adv.*, by nothing.

nihilōminus, *adv.*, nevertheless.

nimis, nimium, *adv.*, too much.

nisi, *conj.*, unless.

nitidus, *adj.*, bright, polished, elegant.

nix, nivis, 3 *f.*, snow.

nōm-en, -inis, 3 *n.*, name.

nōmino, 1, name.

non, *adv.*, not.

nondum, *adv.*, not yet.

nonnihil, *n. indecl.*, something.

nonnullus, *adj.*, some.

nonnumquam, *adv.*, sometimes.

nōs, nostr-um or -i, *c.*, we, us.

nosc-o, -ere, nōvi, nōtum, 3, recognize.

nost-er, -ra, -rum, *adj.*, our.

nota, 1 *f.*, brand, mark.

notābil-is, -e, *adj.*, notable, attracting attention.

notārius, 2 *m.*, shorthand writer.

novus, *adj.*, new, recent.

no-x, -ctis, 3 *f.*, night.

nūb-es, -is, 3 *f.*, cloud.

nūbilus, *adj.*, cloudy.

nullus, *adj.*, no, none.

num, *interrog. partic.*; *in direct questions expecting answer 'no'; in indirect*, whether.

nūm-en, -inis, 3 *n.*, divine being, divine will.

numerus, 2 *m.*, number.

numquam, *adv.*, never.

nunc, *adv.*, now.

nuntio, 1, announce.

nuntius, 2 *m.*, messenger, news.

nūper, *adv.*, lately.

nupta, 1 *f.*, bride.

nuptiae, 1 *f. pl.*, wedding.

nusquam, *adv.*, nowhere.

nūtrio, 4, nourish, nurse.

nūtr-ix, -īcis, 3 *f.*, nurse.

O

ob, *prep. with acc.*, on account of.

oblīquus, *adj.*, slanting, sidelong.

obr-uo, -uere, -ui -ūtum, 3, overwhelm.

obscūrit-ās, -ātis, 3 *f.*, gloom, obscurity.

observo, 1, watch, observe.

ob-sideo, -sidēre, -sēdi, -sessum, 2, sit over against.

obstināti-o, -ōnis, 3 *f.*, obstinacy.

ob-strepo, -strepere, -strepui, -strepitum, 3, make a noise at, disturb.

obstri-ngo, -ngere, -nxi, -ctum, 3, pledge, bind.

obstr-uo, -uere, -uxi, -uctum, 3, obstruct, impede.

ob-tero, -terere, -trīvi, -trītum, 3, crush.

ob-venio, -venīre, -vēni, -ventum, 4, fall in the way of, be left to (of an inheritance).

obversor, 1 dep., hover about, move about near.

occāsi-o, -ōnis, 3 f., opportunity.

occī-do, -dere, -di, -sum, 3, kill.

occultē, adv., secretly.

occupātus, adj., busy.

occur-ro, -rere, -ri, -sum, 3, run to meet, approach, remedy.

octo, numer., eight.

oculus, 2 m., eye.

od-or, -ōris, 3 m., scent, smell.

odōrātus, adj., fragrant.

officiōsus, adj., obliging, dutiful.

officium, 2 n., duty, service.

olea, 1 f., olive.

olīva, 1 f., olive.

omn-is, -e, adj., all.

omnīno, adv., altogether.

opācus, adj., shady.

opera, 1 f., exertion, trouble, effort.

oper-io, -īre, -ui, -tum, 4, cover.

opīmus, adj., fat, sumptuous.

opīnor, 1 dep., suppose.

oppidum, 2 n., town.

op-pleo, -plēre, -plēvi, -plētum, 2, fill completely.

opportūnus, adj., opportune, welcome.

oppr-imo, -imere, -essi, -essum, 3, overthrow.

(ops), opis, 3 f., help, assistance ; pl., opes, wealth.

optimus, superl. of bonus, very good, best.

opto, 1, desire, wish for.

op-us, -eris, 3 n., work, esp. literary work.

ōrārius, 2 m., coasting vessel.

ōrāti-o, -ōnis, 3 f., a speech.

orb-is, -is, 3 m., circle, circular movement, world.

ord-o, -inis, 3 m., order, rank.

or-ior, -īrī, -tus sum, 4 dep., rise.

orno, 1, adorn, embellish, honour ; ornātus, adj., distinguished.

ōro, 1, plead, implore.

ōs, ōris, 3 n., mouth, face.

os, ossis, 3 n., bone.

osten-do, -dere, -di, -sum, 3, show.

ostento, 1, show, display, present.

ostreum, 2 n., oyster.

ōtiōsus, adj., unoccupied, enjoying leisure.

ōtium, 2 n., leisure.

ōvum, 2 n., egg.

P

pacti-o, -ōnis, 3 f., bargain, agreement.

paedagōgus, 2 m., tutor in charge of children going to school.

paene, adv., almost.

paenitentia, 1 f., repentance, second thoughts.

paenit-et, -uit, 2 impers., it repents one.

pānārium, 2 n., bread-basket.

pannus, 2 m., cloth.

pār, paris, *adj.*, equal.

parcus, *adj.*, sparing, thrifty.

paren-s, -tis, 3 *c.*, parent.

pari-es, -etis, 3 *m.*, wall.

par-io, -ere, peperi, partum, 3, bring forth, invent, procure.

paro, 1, prepare.

par-s, -tis, 3 *f.*, portion, part, share.

parsimōnia, 1 *f.*, thrift, frugality.

partim, *adv.*, partly.

parum, *adv.*, too little.

parvulus, *adj.*, very small.

parvus, *adj.*, small.

pascuum, 2 *n.*, pasture.

pastus, 4 *m.*, pasture, fodder.

pat-er, -ris, 3 *m.*, father.

paterfamili-as, -ae, 1 *m.*, householder, head of a family.

paternus, *adj.*, of a father, paternal.

patientia, 1 *f.*, patience, endurance.

pat-ior, -i, passus sum, 3 *dep.*, endure, experience, permit.

patria, 1 *f.*, native land.

patrōnus, 2 *m.*, patron, protector.

pauci, *adj.*, few.

paulo, paulum, *adv.*, a little, by little.

pavimentum, 2 *n.*, pavement.

pect-us, -oris, 3 *n.*, chest.

pecūliār-is, -e, *adj.*, special, extraordinary.

pecūnia, 1 *f.*, money.

pec-us, -oris, 3 *n.*, cattle, herd of cattle.

per, *prep. with acc.*, through, throughout, among, by reason of.

per-ago, -agere, -ēgi, -actum, 3, carry through, accomplish.

perco-quo, -quere, -xi, -ctum, 3, cook, ripen.

percunctor, 1 *dep.*, make close enquiries.

percur-ro, -rere, -ri, -sum, 3, ride or pass rapidly through.

perd-o, -ere, -idi, -itum, 3, lose, waste.

peregrē, *adv.*, abroad.

peregrīnāti-o, -ōnis, 3 *f.*, sojourn or travel abroad.

perenn-is, -e, *adj.*, never failing, everlasting.

per-eo, -īre, -īvi or -ii, -itum, 4, perish, am ruined.

per-fero, -ferre, -tuli, -lātum, 3, bear to the end.

perfidus, *adj.*, faithless, treacherous.

per-fodio, -fodere, -fōdi, -fossum, 3, pierce.

per-fringo, -fringere, -frēgi, -fractum, 3, break up.

Pergamum, 2 *n.*, Pergamum, ancient kingdom of the Attalids in S.E. Asia Minor. Later important Roman town.

per-go, -gere, -rexi, -rectum, 3, proceed, go to.

pergrātus, *adj.*, very agreeable.

perīclitor, 1 *dep.*, run risk.

perīculum, 2 *n.*, danger.

perītē, *adv.*, cunningly, skilfully.

perjūrus, *adj.*, (one) who breaks an oath.

perman-eo, -ēre, -si, -sum, 2, remain to the end.

per-moveo, -movēre, -mōvi, -mōtum, 2, excite, agitate.

perperam, *adv.*, wrongly.

per-petior, -peti, -pessus sum, 3 *dep.*, bear, submit to the end.

perscrī-bo, -bere, -psi, -ptum, 3, write out.

persevēro, 1, persist, persevere.

per-sisto, -sistere, -stiti, —, 3, abide, persist.

person-o, -āre, -ui, -itum, 1, resound.

perst-o, -āre, -iti, -ātum, 1, remain stedfast.

pertinācia, 1 f., persistence, obstinacy.

pertin-eo, -ēre, -ui, —, 2, pertain to, concern.

perturbo, 1, throw into confusion.

pervagor, 1 dep., spread through.

per-venio, -venīre, -vēni, -ventum, 4, arrive, reach.

pessimē, adv., superl. of male, very badly.

pestilen-s, -tis, adj., unhealthy, infected, haunted.

pet-o, -ere, -īvi or -ii, -ītum, 3, ask, seek.

phantasm-a, -atis, 3 n., apparition.

philosophus, 2 m., philosopher.

pingu-is, -e, adj., fertile, luxuriant.

pīnus, 2 and 4 f., pine tree.

piscātōrius, adj., used for fishing, of fishing.

pisc-is, -is, 3 m., fish.

piscor, 1 dep., fish.

placeo, 2, please (with dat.).

plānities, 5 f., plain, level-ground.

plānus, adj., level.

platan-ōn, -ōnis, 3 m., grove of plane trees.

plēnus, adj., full.

plērumque, adv., for the most part.

plūrimus, adj., most, very many.

plūs, plūris, more, sing., subst. (with gen.); pl., adj.

poena, 1 f., penalty.

poēta, 1 m., poet.

pōn-o, -ere, posui, positum, 3, set, place, lay aside.

populār-is, -e, adj., popular, belonging to the people.

populus, 2 m., the people.

por-rigo, -rigere, -rexi, -rectum, 3, spread out, draw, offer.

porticus, 4 f., colonnade.

posc-o, -ere, poposci, —, 3, demand, beg.

pos-sideo, -sidēre, -sēdi, -sessum, 2, possess.

possum, posse, potui, be able.

post, prep. with acc., after, behind; adv., afterwards, behind.

posteā, adv., afterwards.

posterus, adj., coming after, next.

post-pōno, -pōnere, -posui, -positum, 3, postpone.

postquam, conj., after.

postrēmo, adv., at last, finally.

potissimum, adv., especially, above all.

potius, adv., rather.

prae-cēdo, -cēdere, -cessi, -cessum, 3, go before, exceed.

prae-ceps, -cipitis, adj., headlong, impetuous, headstrong.

praecept-or, -ōris, 3 m., instructor, teacher.

prae-cipio, -cipere, -cēpi, -ceptum, 3, get beforehand, instruct.

praecipito, 1, hurry headlong.

praecipuē, adv., especially.

praedium, 2 n., farm, estate.

prae-eo, -īre, -īvi or -ii, -itum, 4, dictate a formula.

prae-sideo, -ēre, -sēdi, —, 2, preside at.

prae-sto, -stāre, -stiti, -stitum, 1, excel, afford, present.

prae-sum, -esse, -fui, be over, be in command of (*with dat.*) ; praesen-s, -tis, *partic.*, present.

praetereā, *adv.*, moreover, besides.

praeteritum (*sc.* tempus), 2 *n.*, the past.

praetextātus, *adj.*, wearing the praetexta, or purple-bordered garment.

praet-or, -ōris, 3 *m.*, praetor, Roman magistrate.

praeval-eo, -ēre, -ui, —, 2, prevail, have most influence.

prae-video, -vidēre, -vīdi, -vīsum, 2, foresee.

prātum, 2 *n.*, meadow.

prāvus, *adj.*, warped, perverse.

precor, 1 *dep.*, pray, implore.

prem-o, -ere, pressi, pressum, 3, press.

pretiōsus, *adj.*, valuable.

pretium, 2 *n.*, price, value.

prīmum, prīmo, *adv.*, at first, first.

prīmus, *adj.*, first.

princ-eps, -ipis, 3 *m.*, prince, principal person, esp. the Emperor.

pri-or, -us, *adj.*, the former.

prīvātus, *adj.*, private, private citizen.

prō, *prep. with abl.*, before, in front of, on behalf of, for, instead of, in comparison with.

proavus, 2 *m.*, great-grandfather.

probāti-o, -ōnis, 3 *f.*, trial, approval.

probus, *adj.*, good, virtuous, upright.

prō-cēdo, -cēdere, -cessi, -cessum, 3, advance, go on (of time).

prōcērit-ās, -ātis, 3 *f.*, tallness, stately presence.

prōcērus, *adj.*, tall.

prōcūrāti-o, -ōnis, 3 *f.*, superintendence, office.

prōdū-co, -cere, -xi, -ctum, 3, bring forward, introduce, extend.

profecti-o, -ōnis, 3 *f.*, departure.

prō-fero, -ferre, -tuli, -lātum, 3, bring out, produce, lengthen.

proficisc-or, -i, profectus sum, 3 *dep.*, set out.

proinde, *adv.*, accordingly.

prōmin-eo, -ēre, -ui, —, 2, jut out, project.

prōmiscuus, *adj.*, common, indiscriminate.

prōmissus, *adj.*, allowed to grow long.

prō-mitto, -mittere, -mīsi, -missum, 3, promise, accept an invitation.

prō-moveo, -movēre, -mōvi, -mōtum, 2, move forward, promote.

prōnuntio, 1, pronounce, give verdict.

prope, *adv.*, almost ; *prep. with acc.*, near.

propius, *adv.*, nearer.

prō-pōno, -pōnere, -posui, -positum, 3, put forward, propose.

proprius, *adj.*, own, especial, proper.

propter, *prep. with acc.*, near, on account of.

prōrēp-o, -ere, -si, -tum, 3, creep forth.

prō-ripio, -ripere, -ripui, -reptum, 3, snatch forth.

prōrogo, 1, protract.

prō-sequor, -sequi, -secūtus sum, 3 *dep.*, follow, pursue.

prospecto, 1, look out on.

prō-spicio, -spicere, -spexi, -spectum, 3, look forth upon, look forward to.

prō-sum, -desse, -fui, benefit.

prō-video, -vidēre, -vīdi, -vīsum, 2, provide, foresee.

prōvincia, 1 *f.*, province.

prōvinciāl-is, -e, *adj.*, belonging to the provinces.

proximus, *adj.*, nearest, next.

prūden-s, -tis, *adj.*, foreseeing, prudent ; prūdenter, *adv.*, prudently.

prūdentia, 1 *f.*, prudence, sagacity.

publicus, *adj.*, of the community, public.

pudīcius, *adv.*, more modestly, more virtuously.

puella, 1 *f.*, virgin, girl.

puellār-is, -e, *adj.*, girlish, belonging to a girl.

puer, pueri, 2 *m.*, boy.

puerīliter, *adv.*, in a boyish or childish fashion, foolishly.

pugillār-es, -ium, 3 *m. pl.*, writing tablets.

pugi-o, -ōnis, 3 *m.*, dagger.

pulch-er, -ra, -rum, *adj.*, fair, beautiful.

pūm-ex, -icis, 3 *m.*, pumice-stone.

pūnio, 4, punish.

puto, 1, think, reckon, consider.

putresc-o, -ere, —, —, 3, rot, moulder, grow septic.

Q

quadrijugus, *adj.*, four-horsed.

quadrirēm-is, -is, 3 *f.*, a vessel having four banks of oars.

quae-ro, -rere, -sīvi, -sītum, 3, seek, inquire.

quāl-is, -e, *adj.*, of what kind, of such a sort as.

quāl-iscumque, -ecumque, *adj.*, of whatever kind.

quam, *adv.*, than; *interrog.*, how ?

quamlibet, *adv.*, however much you please.

quamquam, *conj.*, although (*with indic.*).

quamvis, *adv.* and *conj.*, however much ; *with subj.*, although.

quando, *adv.* and *conj.*, at what time ?

quantulum, *adv.*, how trifling!

quantum, *adv.*, as much as, how much.

quantus, *adj.*, how great, as great as.

quārē, *adv.*, why.

quartus, *adj.*, fourth.

quasi, *adv.* and *conj.*, as if.

quasso, 1, shake violently.

quātenus, *adv.*, how far, to what extent.

quat-io, -ere, —, quassum, 3, shake.

quattuor, *num.*, four.

-que, *enclitic conj.*, and.

quemadmodum, *interrog.* and *rel. adv.*, how.

querella, 1 *f.*, complaint.

quer-or, -i, questus sum, 3 *dep.*, complain.

querulus, *adj.*, inclined to complain, querulous.

qui, quae, quod, *rel. pron.*, who.

quia, *conj.*, because.

quīcumque, quaecumque, quodcumque, *pron.*, whosoever.

quīdam, quaedam, quoddam, *indef. pron.*, a certain.

quidem, *adv.*, indeed, at least ; ne . . . quidem, not even.

qui-es, -ētis, 3 *f.*, quiet, rest.

qui-esco, -escere, -ēvi, -ētum, 3, sink to rest, be still.

quiētus, *adj.*, calm, tranquil.

quīlibet, quaelibet, quodlibet (*subst.* quidlibet), *pron.*, anyone you please.

quin, *conj.*, yea indeed, nay rather ; *with dep. clause*, that not, but that.

quinque, *num.*, five.

quintus, *adj.*, fifth.

quirītātus, 4 *m.*, wailing.

quis, qua, quid, *indef. pron.*, someone, anyone.

quisquam, quidquam, *pron.*, anyone, anything (in negative sentences).

quisque, quaeque, quidque, *indef. pron.*, each.

quisquis, quaequa, quod-quod(*subst.* quidquid),*pron.*, whosoever.

quo, *adv. and conj.*, whither.

quod, *conj.*, as to what, in so far as, because.

quōminus, *conj.*, by which the less, i.e. to the end that not.

quoque, *adv.*, also.

quot, *indecl. adj.*, how many, as many as.

quōusque, *adv.*, how long ?

R

rabidus, *adj.*, raving, enraged.

rāmus, 2 *m.*, branch.

rap-io, -ere, -ui, -tum, 3, seize, snatch.

rāro, *adv.*, seldom.

rārus, *adj.*, rare, seldom found, of loose texture.

rati-o, -ōnis, 3 *f.*, reason, reflection, consideration, reckoning.

re-cipio, -cipere, -cēpi, -ceptum, 3, take back ; sē recipere, retire, retreat.

recito, 1, recite, read out.

recordāti-o, -ōnis, 3 *f.*, recollection.

recreo, 1, renew, revive.

rectus, *adj.*, straight, upright ; rectē, *adv.*, fitly, rightly, wisely.

recub-o, -are, —, —, 1, lie, recline.

red-do, -dere, -didi, -ditum, 3, give back, pay, render, remit.

red-eo, -īre, -īvi or -ii, -itum, 4, come or go back, return.

redormio, -īre, —, —, 4, sleep again.

refer-cio, -cīre, -si, -tum, 4, fill up, stuff.

re-fero, -ferre, -ttuli, -lātum, 3, bring or give back, win, refer, tell a story.

re-fugio, -fugere, -fūgi, —, 3, fly from, flee, escape.

regi-o, -ōnis, 3 *f.*, district, countryside.

rēgius, *adj.*, kingly, regal.

regnum, 2 *n.*, kingdom.

rego, regere, rexi, rectum, 3, rule, direct.

regre-dior, -di, -ssus sum, 3 *dep.*, return.

rē-jicio, -jicere, -jēci, -jectum, 3, reject, vomit (blood).

relātus, 4 *m.*, report.

relēgo, 1, banish.

rel-inquo, -inquere, -īqui, -ictum, 3, leave, abandon.

reliquus, *adj.*, the remaining, the rest of.

reluctor, 1 *dep.*, oppose.

reman-eo, **-ēre**, **-si**, —, 2, stay behind, remain.

re-mitto, **-mittere**, **-mīsi**, **-missum**, 3, remit, give up, slacken.

renuntio, 1, renounce, announce, report.

re-pello, **-pellere**, **-ppuli**, **-pulsum**, 3, drive back.

repentē, *adv.*, suddenly, unexpectedly.

repet-o, **-ere**, **-īvi** or **-ii**, **-ītum**, 3, repeat, seek again.

reporto, 1, bring home.

reprehen-do, **-dere**, **-di**, **-sum**, 3, reprove, chide.

repr-imo, **-imere**, **-essi**, **-essum**, 3, check, control.

reputo, 1, think, consider.

requī-ro, **-rere**, **-sīvi** or **-sii**, **-sītum**, 3, search for, ask, miss.

res, 5 *f.*, thing, matter, estate, property.

rescri-bo, **-bere**, **-psi**, **-ptum**, 3, write back.

resid-o, **-ere**, **resēdī**, —, 3, sit down, abate.

resorb-eo, **-ēre**, —, —, 2, suck back.

re-spicio, **-spicere**, **-spexi**, **-spectum**, 3, look back at, regard, turn attention to.

respon-deo, **-dēre**, **-di**, **-sum**, 2, reply.

responsum, 2 *n.*, answer.

respublica, **reipublicae**, *f.*, the state, community.

retardo, 1, keep back, check, discourage.

rēt-e, **-is**, 3 *n.*, net.

re-tineo, **-tinēre**, **-tinui**, **-tentum**, 2, keep back, retain.

retracto, 1, handle again, revise.

reus, 2 *m.*, defendant; *also adj.*

rever-tor, **-ti**, **-sus sum**, 3 *dep.*, return.

revoco, 1, call back, detain.

revol-vo, **-vere**, **-vi**, **-ūtum**, 3, roll back.

rex, **rēgis**, 3 *m.*, king.

rī-deo, **-dēre**, **-si**, **-sum**, 2, laugh at, smile.

rīdiculus, *adj.*, laughable, absurd.

rīpa, 1 *f.*, bank.

rīsus, 4 *m.*, laugh, smile.

rīte, *adv.*, duly, properly.

rīvus, 2 *m.*, stream.

rōbustus, *adj.*, strong, robust.

rogo, 1, interrogate, ask for.

rūga, 1 *f.*, wrinkle.

ruīna, 1 *f.*, collapse, downfall.

rūm-or, **-ōris**, 3 *m.*, rumour.

rursus, *adv.*, again.

rū-s, **-ris**, 3 *n.*, the country (as opposed to town).

rusticus, *adj.*, in or belonging to the country.

S

sacra, 2 *n. pl.*, rites.

sacrāmentum, 2 *n.*, solemn oath.

saeculum, 2 *n.*, age, epoch.

saepe, *adv.*, often.

saevitia, 1 *f.*, cruelty, barbarity.

saevus, *adj.*, cruel.

salto, 1, dance vigorously.

salūbr-is, **-e**, *adj.*, healthy.

sal-ūs, **-ūtis**, 3 *f.*, safety.

salūto, 1, greet.

salvus, *adj.*, safe, kept safe.

sanctus, *adj.*, pious, holy.

sānē, *adv.*, exceedingly, certainly.

sangu-is, **-inis**, 3 *m.*, blood.

sānit-ās, **-ātis**, 3 *f.*, sanity, health.

sānus, *adj.*, sane, healthy.

sapienter, *adv.,* wisely, sensibly.

sapientia, 1 *f.,* wisdom.

sap-io, -ere, -īvi or **-ii, —,** 3, have taste, discernment.

sarcina, 1 *f.,* package, luggage.

sarcinula, 1 *f.,* little bundle.

satis, *adv.,* enough ; *comp.* **satius,** preferable, better.

Sāturnāli-a, -ōrum, 2 *n. pl.,* festival of the Saturnalia (December 17th).

scel-us, -eris, 3 *n.,* crime.

sc-io, -īre, -īvi or **-ii, -ītum,** 4, know.

scrī-bo, -bere, -psi, -ptum, 3, write.

sē, sui, *pron. reflex.,* himself, herself, themselves.

sēcessus, 4 *m.,* retreat, retirement.

sec-o, -āre, -ui, -tum, 1, cut off, divide, traverse.

sector, 1 *dep.,* follow.

secundum, *prep. with acc.,* in accordance with.

secundus, *adj.,* favourable ; **secundae res,** prosperity.

sēcūrit-ās, -ātis, 3 *f.,* tranquillity, freedom from anxiety.

sed, *conj.,* but.

sed-eo, -ēre, sēdi, sessum, 2, be seated, sit.

sēdulo, *adv.,* carefully.

segn-is, -e, *adj.,* lazy, sluggish.

sella, 1 *f.,* seat, sedan-chair.

semel, *adv.,* once.

semper, *adv.,* always.

senātus, 4 *m.,* senate.

sen-ex, -is, 3, *noun or adj.,* old man, old ; *comp.,* **seni-or, -ōris,** older, rather old.

sententia, 1 *f.,* opinion, view.

sen-tio, -tīre, -si, -sum, 4, perceive, feel.

sep-elio, -elīre, -elīvi or **-elii, -ultum,** 4, bury.

septem, *numer.,* seven.

septimus, *adj.,* seventh.

septingent-i, -ōrum, *adj.,* seven hundred.

se-quor, -qui, -cūtus sum, 3 *dep.,* follow.

serēnus, *adj.,* clear, cloudless, calm.

sērio, *adv.,* in earnest.

serm-o, -ōnis, 3 *m.,* talk, conversation.

serp-o, -ere, -si, -tum, 3, creep, spread.

servo, 1, keep, observe, save.

servulus, 2 *m.,* young slave.

servus, 2 *m.,* slave.

sevērit-ās, -ātis, 3 *f.,* sternness, strictness.

sextus, *adj.,* sixth.

sexus, 4 *m.,* sex.

sī, *conj.,* if.

sic, *adv.,* thus, so.

sicco, 1, dry.

siccus, *adj.,* dry.

sīcut, *adv.,* just as.

significo, 1, show, indicate.

signo, 1, sign, attest.

signum, 2 *n.,* mark, standard, statue.

silentium, 2 *n.,* silence.

silva, 1 *f.,* wood, forest.

simil-is, -e, *adj.,* similar to, like.

simplicit-ās, -ātis, 3 *f.,* frankness, simplicity.

simpliciter, *adv.,* frankly.

simul, *adv.,* at the same time.

simulācrum, 2 *n.,* effigy.

simulo, 1, pretend.

sincērus, *adj.,* genuine, pure.

sine, *prep. with abl.,* without.

singul-i, -ae, -a, *adj.,* individual, separate.

sinist-er, -ra, -rum, *adj.,* on the left, unlucky, adverse.

sīph-o, -ōnis, 3 *m.,* small pipe, fire-engine.

sī-quis, -qua, -quid, *indef. pron.,* if anyone, anything.

sist-o, -ere, stiti, statum, 3, check, stop, stand.

situs, 4 *m.,* position, situation.

sīve, seu, whether ; **sīve . . . sīve,** whether . . . or.

sōl, sōlis, 3 *m.,* sun.

sōlācium, 2 *n.,* consolation.

solea, 1 *f.,* sole, sandal.

sol-eo, -ēre, -itus sum, 2 *semidep.,* be accustomed.

solidus, *adj.,* firm.

sōlitūd-o, -inis, 3 *f.,* solitude, deserted place.

sollemn-is, -e, *adj.,* yearly, customary, solemn.

sollicitē, *adv.,* with anxiety, anxiously.

sollicito, 1, disturb, attract.

sollicitūd-o, -inis, 3 *f.,* anxiety.

sollicitus, *adj.,* careful.

sōlus, *adj.,* alone, only.

sol-vo, -vere, -vi, -ūtum, 3, loosen, pay.

somnus, 2 *m.,* sleep.

sonan-s, -tis, *adj.,* loud, crashing.

son-o, -āre, -ui, -itum, 1, sound.

sonus, 2 *m.,* sound.

spar-go, -gere, -si, -sum, 3, scatter, sprinkle.

spatiōsus, *adj.,* spacious, commodious.

spatium, 2 *n.,* space (of distance or time).

species, 5 *f.,* appearance, a particular sort.

spectāculum, 2 *n.,* public entertainment, spectacle.

spectāt-or, -ōris, 3 *m.,* spectator.

specto, 1, look at, examine.

spēro, 1, hope.

spes, 5 *f.,* hope.

spīritus, 4 *m.,* breath, breeze, life.

splendidus, *adj.,* distinguished.

sponsāli-a, -um, 3 *n. pl.,* betrothal.

squāl-or, -ōris, 3 *m.,* filth, dirty garments.

squilla, 1 *f.,* lobster.

stabil-is, -e, *adj.,* firm, stable.

stagnum, 2 *n.,* pool, lagoon.

statim, *adv.,* immediately.

status, *adj.,* fixed.

stilus, 2 *m.,* pen.

sto, stāre, steti, statum, 1, stand.

stomachus, 2 *m.,* digestion, windpipe.

strangulo, 1, strangle, suffocate.

strepitus, 4 *m.,* noise, rattling

stri-ngo, -ngere, -nxi, -ctum, 3, draw (from sheath)

stud-eo, -ēre, -ui, —, 2, study.

studiōsus, *adj.,* studious, busy.

studium, 2 *n.,* study, zeal, pursuit.

suā-deo, -dēre, -si, -sum, 2, persuade, advise, suggest.

suāvit-ās, -ātis, 3 *f.,* charm.

sub, *prep. with acc. and abl.,* under, beneath.

sub-eo, -īre, -ii, -itum, 4, undergo, approach, occur.

sub-icio, -icere, -jēci, -jectum, put below ; **subicere oculis,** look down upon.

subjac-eo, -ēre, -ui, —, 2, lie under or near.

subjectus, *adj.*, stretched below.

sub-ruo, -ruere, -rui, -rūtum, 3, undermine, overthrow.

sub-sisto, -sistere, -stiti, —, 3, stop, stay.

sub-sum, -esse, -fui, be near.

subtīl-is, -e, *adj.*, acute, clever, having good taste.

suburbānus, *adj.*, suburban ; **suburbanum** *sc.* **praedium,** country house.

suf-ficio, -ficere, -fēci, -fectum, 3, suffice.

sulp-ur, -uris, 3 *n.*, sulphur.

sum, esse, fui, be.

summa, 1 *f.*, chief point, crisis.

summus, *adj.*, topmost, greatest, supreme.

sūm-o, -ere, -psi, -ptum, 3, take, assume.

sumptuōsius, *adv.*, too extravagantly, at too high a price.

sumptus, 4 *m.*, expense.

supell-ex, -ectilis, 3 *f.*, furniture.

super, *prep. with acc. or abl.*, at, over.

superbus, *adj.*, proud, haughty.

super-fundo, -fundere, -fūdi, -fūsum, 3, pour over.

supero, 1, overcome, surpass.

superst-es, -itis, *adj.*, surviving.

superstiti-o, -ōnis, 3 *f.*, religious belief, superstition.

supplicium, 2 *n.*, punishment.

supplico, 1, make petition, pray (*with dat.*).

suprēmus, *adj.*, supreme, final, last.

sur-go, -gere, -rexi, -rectum, 3, arise.

sus-cipio, -cipere, -cēpi, -ceptum, 3, undertake, take up.

suspen-do, -dere, -di, -sum, 3, hang up, keep in suspense.

sus-picio, -picere, -pexi, -pectum, 3, look up to, respect, suspect.

suus, *adj. reflex.*, his, her or its own.

T

tabula, 1 *f.*, writing tablet ; *plur.*, account, will.

tāl-is, -e, *adj.*, such, of such quality.

tam, *adv.*, so, so much.

tamen, *conj.*, however.

tamquam, *adv.*, as if.

tandem, *adv.*, at last, finally.

tang-o, -ere, tetigi, tactum, 3, touch, reach.

tanto, *adv.*, so much, so greatly.

tantulus, *adj.*, so small.

tantum, *adv.*, only.

tantus, *adj.*, so great.

tardus, *adj.*, slow, dull ; **tardē** (*comp.* **tardius**), *adv.*, slowly.

tectum, 2 *n.*, roof ; *pl.*, dwellings.

temperies, 5 *f.*, mildness, temper.

tempest-ās, -ātis, 3 *f.*, weather, storm.

templum, 2 *n.*, temple.

temp-us, -oris, 3 *n.*, time.

ten-ax, -ācis, *adj.*, tenacious, steadfast.

tend-o, -ere, tetendi, tensum or **tentum,** 3, stretch, tend, steer.

tenebr-ae, -ārum, 1 *f. pl.*, gloom, darkness.

ten-eo, -ēre, -ui, -tum, 2, keep, hold, restrain.

tener, -a, -um, *adj.*, tender, delicate.

tenuo, 1, make thin.

tep-or, -ōris, 3 *m.*, warmth.

ter-go, -gere, -si, -sum, 3, dry.

tergum, 2 *n.,* back ; **a tergo,** from behind, behind.

tern-i, -ae, -a, *adj.,* three each.

terra, 1 *f.,* earth, land.

tertius, *adj.,* third.

testāmentum, 2 *n.,* will.

Tiberīnus, *adj.,* on the Tiber.

Tiber-is, -is, 3 *f.,* Tiber, river on which Rome stands.

Tifernum, 2 *n.,* small Roman town on the Tiber.

timeo, 2, fear.

tim-or, -ōris, 3 *m.,* fear, panic.

titulus, 2 *m.,* placard, bill.

toga, 1 *f.,* outer garment of a Roman civilian.

toll-o, -ere, sustuli, sublātum, 3, raise, exalt.

tormentum, 2 *n.,* torture.

torqu-eo, -ēre, torsi, tortum, 2, twist, rack, pain.

torus, 2 *m.,* couch, bed.

tot, *adj. indecl.,* so many.

tōtus, *adj.,* all, entire.

trab-s or **trab-es, -is,** 3 *f.,* beam, timber.

tractātus, 4 *m.,* treatment, discussion.

tracto, 1, handle, treat.

trād-o, -ere, -idi, -itum, 3, hand over, give up, bequeath.

tra-ho, -here, -xi, -ctum, 3, draw, protract.

trām-es, -itis, 3 *m.,* side-path, way.

trans-eo, -īre, -īvi or **-ii, -itum,** 4, go over, pass by.

trans-fero, -ferre, -tuli, -lātum, 3, transfer.

trans-mitto, -mittere, -mīsi, -missum, 3, spend.

trecent-i, -ae, -a, *adj.,* three hundred.

trem-or, -ōris, 3 *m.,* a trembling, quaking

trepido, 1, tremble, be panic stricken.

trēs, tria, *gen.* **trium,** *adj.,* three.

triennium, 2 *n.,* period of three years.

trīgintā, *numer. adj.,* thirty.

trist-is, -e, *adj.,* sad, mournful.

truncus, 2 *m.,* trunk.

tū, tui, *pron.,* thou, you.

tum, *adv.,* then.

tum-or, -ōris, 3 *m.,* swelling, commotion.

tunc, *adv.,* then.

tunica, 1 *f.,* dress.

turba, 1 *f.,* crowd.

turpissimē, *adv.,* most discreditably.

tūs, tūris, 3 *n.,* frankincense.

Tusc-i, -ōrum, 2 *m. pl.,* ancient tribe of Tuscany, later used for Tuscany.

tussicula, 1 *f.,* slight cough.

tūtus, *adj.,* safe, secure.

tuus, *adj.,* thy.

Tyrius, *adj.,* Tyrian ; **(so)** purple (from the Tyrian dye).

U

ubi, *adv.,* where, when.

ubīque, *adv.,* everywhere.

ulc-us, -eris, 3 *n.,* ulcer, sore.

ullus, *adj.,* any.

ulter-ior, -ius, *adj.,* further, more distant.

ultimus, *adj.,* last.

ulti-o, -ōnis, 3 *f.,* revenge.

ultrā, *adv.* and *prep. with acc.,* beyond, past.

ululātus, 4 *m.,* wailing, lamentation.

umbra, 1 *f.,* shade, shadow.

umquam, *adv.,* ever.

ūnā, *adv.,* together.

unde, *adv.,* whence.

undique, *adv.*, from or on all sides.

un-go, -gere, -xi, -ctum, 3, anoint.

unguentum, 2 *n.*, ointment.

ūniversus, *adj.*, general ; in ūniversum, in general.

ūnus, *adj.*, one, alone.

urbānus, *adj.*, of the city, devoted to city life, sophisticated.

urb-s, -is, 3 *f.*, city.

usquam, *adv.*, anywhere.

usque, *adv.*, all the while ; usque ad, even to.

ut, *adv.*, where, how, as, when ; *conj.*, so that, in order that.

uterque, utraque, utrumque, *pron. and adj.*, each of two, both.

ūt-or, -i, ūsus sum, 3 *dep.*, use, enjoy (*with abl.*).

utrimque, *adv.*, on both sides.

utrum, *interrog. adv.*, whether.

ux-or, -ōris, 3 *f.*, wife.

V

vaco, 1, have leisure for, attend to (*with dat.*).

vacuus, *adj.*, unoccupied, empty.

valē, *imper. of* valeo, farewell.

valētūd-o, -inis, 3 *f.*, state of health, illness.

vānus, *adj.*, idle, vain.

variet-ās, -ātis, 3 *f.*, variety.

varius, *adj.*, various, varied.

vastus, *adj.*, huge, violent.

-ve, *enclitic conj.*, or.

vehementer, *adv.*, violently, earnestly, very much.

vehiculum, 2 *n.*, carriage.

ve-ho, -here, -xi, -ctum, 3, carry ; *in pass.*, drive, sail.

vel . . . vel, either . . . or.

vēlōcit-ās, -ātis, 3 *f.*, speed.

velut, *adv.*, just as.

vēna, 1 *f.*, vein.

vēnābulum, 2 *n.*, hunting spear.

vēnāti-o, -ōnis, 3 *f.*, hunting, chase.

ven-do, -dere, -didi, -ditum, 3, sell.

vēn-eo, -īre, -īvi or -ii, -itum, 4, am sold, am up for sale.

veneror, 1 *dep.*, reverence.

venia, 1 *f.*, consideration, pardon.

ven-io, -īre, vēni, ventum, 4, come.

vēnor, 1 *dep.*, hunt.

vent-er, -ris, 3 *m.*, stomach.

ventōsus, *adj.*, windy.

ventus, 2 *m.*, wind.

verbero, 1, beat.

verbum, 2 *n.*, word.

verēcundia, 1 *f.*, modesty.

verēcundus, *adj.*, modest.

vērit-ās, -ātis, 3 *f.*, truth, honesty.

vernus, *adj.*, vernal, spring-like.

versus, 4 *m.*, verse, line.

ver-to, -tere, -ti, -sum, 3, turn.

vērus, *adj.*, true, genuine ; vērē, *adv.*, really, rightly ; vērō, *adv.*, actually, indeed, but ; vērum etiam, but also.

vespera, 1 *f.*, evening.

vest-er, -ra, -rum, *adj.*, your.

vestīgium, 2 *n.*, footprint ; in eōdem vestīgio, in the same place.

vestio, 4, clothe, cover.

vest-is, -is, 3 *f.*, clothing.

vet-o, -āre, -ui, -itum, 1, forbid, oppose.

vet-us, -eris, *adj.*, old, ancient.

vexo, 1, harass, embarrass.

via, 1 *f.*, way, road.

viāticum, 2 *n.*, journey-money.

vīcīnus, *adj.*, neighbouring.
victima, 1 *f.*, victim.
vict-or, -ōris, 3 *m.*, winner, victor.
victus, 4 *m.*, subsistence, livelihood.
vīcus, 2 *m.*, hamlet.
vid-eo, -ēre, vīdi, vīsum, 2, see, look at ; *passive*, seem.
vigilantia, 1 *f.*, wakefulness, vigilance.
vigilia, 1 *f.*, wakefulness, insomnia.
vigilo, 1, be awake, watch.
vīginti, *numer.*, twenty.
vig-or, -ōris, 3 *m.*, vigour.
vīlit-ās, -ātis, 3 *f.*, cheapness.
villa, 1 *f.*, country-house or estate.
vinculum, 2 *n.*, chain, bond.
vīnea, 1 *f.*, vineyard.
vīnum, 2 *n.*, wine.
viola, 1 *f.*, violet.
violentia, 1 *f.*, force, violence.
vir, viri, 2 *m.*, male, man.
vīr-es, -ium, 3 *f. pl.*, strength, powers.
virgināl-is, -e, *adj.*, maidenly.

virid-is,-e, *adj.*, green, vigorous.
virīl-is, -e, *adj.*, of a man, manly.
vīta, 1 *f.*, life.
vīvidus, *adj.*, lifelike, lively, vivid.
vī-vo, -vere, -xi, -ctum, 3, live.
voco, 1, call.
volo, velle, volui, —, 1, wish, be willing.
volūm-en, -inis, 3 *n.*, volume, scroll.
volupt-ās, -ātis, 3 *f.*, pleasure.
vōs, vestr-um or -i, *pron.*, you, ye.
vox, vōcis, 3 *f.*, voice, elocution.
vulg-us, -i, 2 *n.*, the common people, the masses.
vuln-us, -eris, 3 *n.*, wound.
vultus, 4 *m.*, face, expression ; compōnere vultum, put on a serious expression.

X

xeni-a, -ōrum, 2 *n. pl.*, gifts accorded to a guest.
xystus, 2 *m.*, colonnade, terrace.